Incognito

Erin L. Monaghan

DEDICATION

Dedicated to a friend;
My best friend.
Who may be a little yellow, and blue, pink, and red.
Torn around some of the edges.
Been my friend a long time.
Or a short time, depending on how you look at it.
Nonetheless,
A good friend.
A really, really good friend.
Thanks for being there for me.

CONTENTS

Acknowledgments

Erin L. Monaghan

ACKNOWLEDGMENTS

I most importantly want to thank a very special person who is an outstanding genius. But I will disclose her name right now, so you can just focus on her. She is the sole purpose why I wrote the book in the first place. Because of her- this glorious girl- I wrote it. I only had the month of November to write it, so you can imagine- I was under a time crunch. But she helped me through it, and that's why I chose to do it so quickly. She was able to give me the constructive criticism I needed throughout the whole entire writing process. She even gave me the few extra pushes I needed while writing into the later part of the nights when my brain felt fried, but she knew I needed to get it done. She also helped give me ideas for the book. And I just wanted to acknowledge her. Thank you Me.

PREFACE

I was in a room, surrounded by nothing.

The blank colored walls were surrounded by nothing.

The table I was sitting at was surrounded by nothing, expect for a peculiar woman with bad taste in fashion sitting directly in front of it. She handed me a circular mirror and asked me to gaze in it, and to tell her what I saw

But I saw nothing.

I kept looking harder and a face appeared: my face. It looked like me, with the same messy brown hair that couldn't decide if it wanted to be curly or straight; with the same changing eyes of blue and green, that reminded me of a sea; with the same white face and rosy cheeks that made me look like a clown.

I don't think I saw what she wanted me to see, so I told her that I saw me; the same me that I saw last year; the same me that I have always seen. But she didn't like what I saw.

She tore the mirror from my hand and called me some ugly words that I would never repeat. She yelled at me and hounded me with questions about a boy named Samuel, whom I did in fact know, but wasn't going to say a thing; therefore I endured several hours of this woman screaming at me.

The woman stood up from the chair, frazzled. Her once tamed hair was now sticking out in every direction; her shirt that had once been tucked into her skirt was completely pulled up and out, dangling below her butt. She paced the small room we were in, muttering to herself about the punishment I was going to get when she finished, but In reality, I did nothing wrong. She was to blame; the government was to blame; everybody that had helped push where my world is today was all wrong.

The woman knocked on the old door in the corner of the room, and too guards appeared. She pointed towards me, and muttered a few things to the guards, where they started grabbing my arms. Then they pulled me down the hall, into a cell, and left me.

Now I was in a different room, surrounded by nothing.

The walls that surrounded me were a color of nothing.

Now I was sitting on a small bed, instead of chair to a table, which was surrounded by nothing.

I didn't have the woman though on the bright side to this dull room. But I could hear her laugh echoing through the halls, and I could almost hear myself laughing too.

In this society, you have to be in the wrong to be in the right; now that's screwed up.

CHAPTER 1.

There are some things in life that are not permitted to be talked about. It is possibly one of the most difficult concepts to deal with, especially when your mind is swimming with questions that you cannot ask, and answers that you do not want. But eventually, it gets a little bit easier.

It becomes easier to block out the stupid remarks people make, just simply because society simply tells them to.

It becomes easier to go with the flow, even when you don't want to.

I remember the first time I had asked my mom what a boy was. It was one of the most terrifying experiences that I encountered as a child, because normally children were generally well behaved, and there were hardly any outbursts. Moms of this generation were strict and stern and taught their children well enough to be polite, to ask someone how they were, to say please, and thank you.

But I remember clear as day what happened, and if looks could kill, I swore my mom would have had my funeral right in the middle of that festival, the place where I had asked her the question.

~

"Mom," I said, and tugged on her elbow. The floats of the victorious women from the Women's Revolution were strolling down the street, the crowd cheering them on; I didn't think she had heard me, so I tried once more.

"Mom, I have a question," I said again, this time more loudly.

"Yes." She looked down to me, her brown eyes looking somewhat puzzled. I didn't often ask questions.

"What does a boy mea-" I hadn't had time to finish

7

my question when heads started turning towards me.

Screams echoed from several bystanders, but luckily it didn't alert everybody; they attention was glued to the yellow balloons and floats that were passing by. The people were also going deaf from the loudness of the parade; however, it did alarm my mom even more, so she yanked me in front of her and shoved her hand in front of my mouth.

"Should we call the cops?"

"Poor child, she's so young, yet her brain has already begun the process of retaliation."

My mom's hand was getting hotter as her grip on my shoulder tightened while the people around us shouted the comments.

She screamed, "She's just a child, everybody. No worries," to calm some people down, which did work. The people surrounding us shifted their focus back to what was more important, the parade.

She bent down so that her mouth was at the height of my ears, which was a big stretch considering how short I was, and put her lips to my ear, and said, "move".

She held onto my arm and dragged me to the outskirts of the crowd, and we left. As we walked down the road to go back home, her brown eyes were a mix of surprise and fear. The road we were walking down was the main strip through my quarter; she never took her eyes off the road. Every now and then her head would tilt down slightly to see me, but then they would return back to the road.

We didn't pass many people, because most of them were at the Women's Revolution Day celebration, but we did pass one creepy cop lady who came up to us.

"Hello, Miss. How are we today?" The cop asked my mom. Her dark orange pants and shirt were spotted with dirt, and her handcuffs were gone. I think my mom had noticed that too.

"Fine, thanks." My mom pushed through the cop, with me still attached to her arm, and tried to get us back to the house.

"Hold on, hold on." She set her arm on my mom so that we would face her again. "Why aren't you at the festival?" The cop's black eyes squared us up, eyeing our tops of our heads to the bottom most bottom of our feet.

I was only six at the time, and not even in school yet, but I did recognize that the cop was acting a little suspicious of something, like we had committed a crime. The cop put her dirty arms on her hips, tapping her foot on the ground violently.

"I could ask you the same thing," my mom said coolly. She smiled slightly, and we turned our backs to the cop and walked straight home; we stopped for nothing.

When we finally reached our rectangular home, with the curtains pulled over the windows, we went inside, and my mom looked at me angrily and asked, "Where did you hear the word boy?"

~

I haven't forgotten that day at all. Not the worried looks from all the other women crowding us, or the way my mom grabbed me with her trembling hands. I never had a chance to answer where I heard that word from, but she wouldn't have liked the answer, now or then; it was my mom. I heard the word boy from my mom, and ever since, I have been obsessed with it.

My mom has never brought that memory up, and neither have I. I think we both keep it locked up for a reason, somewhere safe inside so we do not fall into the horrors of reality; however, it has never stopped me from going to the festival. But most people attend anyway. It is one of the most valued and honored event that takes place every year in May that my subdivision has the opportunity to holding it. The people that you will never find at this celebration are people in the facilities. but otherwise, there is absolutely no reason to not attend.

The Women's Revolution began in the year 2017 when women all over the United States (today it is called First Division) started feeling like they had no place in society. They were being discriminated against even more than they had before; most of the complaints that groups were complaining about were how they were getting paid less to their male counter parts, and not being able to participate higher ranking jobs in the military or fight for their land. Gender roles, too, were becoming such an issue that the revolution is all they had left, according to Christy Labelle.

The numbers of the women who were getting more upset were rising in alarming rates. Eventually there was more than seventy percent of the women who didn't like what was happening, so they started plotting against the guys; their plan was to take down all the men and to get rid of them with the exceptions of the really smart ones. But the government doesn't allow the kind of information we need to know about that issue, so were just taught ' the smart ones', even though I believe it to be different.

Rumors started spreading about the women getting together and building up an army big enough to wipe the males out, but the men were too stupid to even think for a second that the women were capable of such a thing; the men were wrong.

The women of the revolution kept to themselves, and did a phenomenal job. Today, it is unimaginable to how they accomplished it. Women were stealing formulas and secretes about the government, about how to operate weapons of mass destruction, about how to get millions of men to listen to them. But most of them were working in the scientific field of study; and after four long years, it worked.

They started with eliminating the higher power of people, like the president and the secret service, and slowly, and cautiously worked their way form there. When the men decided that the women had gone far too out of control and when enough men had been sacrificed, they started to listen. They surrendered willingly to the women, and now they finally had control.

The main woman that started the whole revolution was Christy Labelle, who is now everybody's savior, and whom everybody prays to.

She was responsible for making sure that the most intelligent men were safe, that way the society in which we all live in could continue. These men from over a century ago would teach all the younger men, who in return would teach the generations below them.

The main subject that we really learn about in school is all about the Women's Revolution. It is always the topic of the month, the week, the day; I know all about it.

In history my teachers constantly talk about continents and country's and about their inhabitants which is shocking to me, because country? That's not even a name.

My teachers say that history has a tendency to repeat itself. But does it? I constantly ask that question, and all the people I know say no. But history is long gone; the women's revolution has blossomed into a "new and better world where the society can and will prosper far greater than it's previous ways, now that the impurities have been removed from it," according to the Establishment of Rights that the founders of Women's Revolution.

I am very limited today to what I am allowed to know about my worlds history. This is the Head of First Division's way of depleting our minds of nonsense for rebellion and uproars and embellishing the great new inventive ways of this new world.

Geographically, the United States exists, but since the revolution, it has been renamed to First Division. The states have completely vanished as well. First Division is divided up into thirty-seven subdivisions that correspond to the areas that joined in the First Division.

The impurities that are written down into the Establishment of Rights pertain to males. They have been completely removed out of society (at least in First Division). They all live in facilities around First Division secluded from life and living free.

So much of today

But instead of saying I live in the first division, I wish I could say that I live in the United States; I would never say it out loud though. I would be put into prison, or my face would be all over the news, or both. Saying what you believe in is not an option in my world now; however, saying what the government believes in while putting on a pretty face is acceptable, even if you don't mean it.

The only time that specific information from the Women's Revolution is talked about is spoken in school. The information leaves the teachers and enters the students where the students may do with it in which they please, only if it stays contained inside.

I can only say that talking about the past is awkward. The teachers seldom make comments about what we say, but they are probably just worried that someone might hear what they actually think; I know I would be.

And maybe one the most important subjects that should never be spoken freely about are where babies come from. I think in the old times – before the revolution- it would be called a sin if a person talked about where babies come from. If the government catches you speaking about it openly, the consequences are brutal. The punishment people can get very, but it usually ends in death, or pretty close to it.

My mom had told me about the baby legend before,

which, as legend has it, says that babies come from both a man and a woman. My mom started talking to me once on a train about the baby legend, but then had shut her mouth as quickly as she let the words man and woman roll off her tongue, in fear that someone had heard our conversation.

I guess nobody heard us because she wasn't taken from me, but I will never know. I can only assume.

In the first division, the government is split up into two pieces, sort of like it was many years ago. In my history class, I learned that it was Republicans and Democrats, but now it is the Searchers and the Supporters. But instead of having the conservatives or liberals, it's just the two.

The baby legend is what the searchers believe in, that there are other ways to make a child. These people are usually easy to tell who they are because they seldom talk about the baby booster procedure. Usually you can find these people talking in secrecy, and only talking to fellow searchers'.

The baby booster is what the supporters believe in, that when a woman falls within the appropriate range to have a child, she is allowed to receive the injection that makes her belly round to have a baby. The first division claims its at its finest ever, and is pleading the women who can have to children to have them.

But I don't believe in that. I think its stupid to make women have children if she doesn't want to have them, and the worst part is, I only have one more year to go until I am eligible to participate, like it's some kind of game.

The facilities are the most dangerous subject to talk about. It essentially is this large open land that is gated, that has a building that is above ground, and below ground. It contains all the men in a specific area, and keeps them there.

I have never personally seen one before, but I have seen several pictures, and heard stories about them. The older girls that went the first year that allowed this fieldtrip said when they went to go visit them; they were nothing like she thought. The gates were extremely tall, gray, dull, and electric, and could sense humans drawing closer to them. She even said that if people got too close to it, the gates would sense it, and told me the gate would start sending electric pulses to you. The pulses would gradually become more painful as the person got nearer to it. The building, as she recalls, was guarded with two to three guards at every entrance or exit, and all the guys in the building wear special bracelets. In essence, the facilities are like jails; the guys get three meals a day, they work certain jobs, and get recreational time.

During your senior year, seniors get to visit the facility in their subdivision. It is required for all seniors to do so, so that all of us can see why we need to keep stand at where we are. To see how guys are so controllable, ignorant, how their power and thoughts do not matter in our society, that it is just a figment of their imagination.

"Sam?"

"Sam? Listen to ME!"

CHAPTER 2.

My head pulled up from my desk while my tired eyes tried to re-focus. My teacher was calling on me.

"Yes?" I said sarcastically. I was in a bad mood today, and I didn't feel like talking much.

Ms. B looked out of breath, and nervous; the beads of sweat on her forehead were dripping so that her curly blonde hair was falling straight, and her pale skin was glistening in the light above. She was walking around in a straight line in front of the classroom eyeing me down; she looked cruel.

"What is Women's Revolution Day?" she questioned me as she pointed her chin in the air. I don't know what made her ask that question either, considering all of us kids grow up knowing about it, but she did, and I told her.

"It's the day where we celebrate women," I said to her. And then I told her everything about it; about the parade of floats of the women that our subdivision has, about the yellow balloons that signify happiness and the victory of our women from over a century ago, about the thousands of women that cheer for the floats, and the hundreds of women that help make the floats.

Ms. B nodded her head as I told her everything, and started writing words on the white board at the head of the class. Her writing was smudged.

"Wrong," she snarled. "It is the day that we honor the great women of our past that helped bring women into power and make our future." And then she finished writing on the board.

"But I guess you were close," she added, with a wide nasty grin. Her lips were thin, but even thinner when she smiled. Then she wrote my name down on the white board and put an X beside it.

"This, class," she paused while motioning her hand in my direction, "is why we do not fall asleep in class. Marks will be taken off, Sam."

The board behind her had field trip written on it, as

well as the facility, and the dates that we would be leaving. My stomach rose with butterflies, and the same thing must have happened to several other girls in my class, because many hands shot in the air quickly, and soon the whole class was shouting questions toward Ms. B.

"Before I answer your questions, let me explain." She started walking around the rows of tables and distributing envelopes to us.

"The facilities are a dangerous subject, as you all know. We do not speak of the facilities unless we are talking about Women's Revolution Day, or if you have a higher job where it requires you to speak of it, like in the government. But because you girls are seniors, and you're taking the annual trip down to one of the facilities, permission has been granted."

She went back up to the head of the classroom, and began again.

"In a few weeks, you will all be heading to the facility of our subdivision called Incognito. You will be there for eleven days where you will observe the males. Note that this is an opportunity in which you will most likely never have again, so it would be impertinent of you to act silly, and abuse this opportunity.

"While you are there, you will be interacting with them by spending every waking moment with them. Your job is to record everything that happens, and to record it down.

"After the eleven days, you will come back here, where you will have to write an essay about your experience. The topic question is how males have every right to be in the facility.

" The essays will be narrowed down after they are turned in. The students with the top five scores will go back to Incognito to further your research with a question of your own in which I will grade. The winning essay will be read at the festival for Women's Day in May. Now," she paused. "Do you girls have any questions?"

The girls with their hands up before MS. B started speaking raised them once again, rising out of their seats as they did so. A girl named Mary was called on.

"My mom says that I am not allowed to go to a facility," she bossily stated. "She doesn't want me mixing with *those animals.*"

Her brown hair was to her shoulders, straight as a line, her jaw line extending out further than most of the girls in our class. Her arms were wrapped up in her chest, as if she was right.

"It has been cleared, Mary. You don't need to worry about it. This field trip is mandatory for all seniors. Your mom can take that up with the government if she'd like, but you will still be going. Yes Rebecca."

Rebecca was a small, quiet girl who sits in the back and never talks. This was new for her. "Is it dangerous? My older sister said it was, and that-"

"No. It is dangerous if you disobey the rules in the facility. They are very strict with who goes in there, but if you follow what the director says, there should be no issue-"

"Ms. B, I have heard that you love going to the facilities, and that you keep in touch with some of them. Is this true?" Amanda interrupted. She spoke very loudly and firmly, so that the whole class could hear. Ms. B started sweating again, and she spoke with a stutter.

"I- I do not g-go th-there for pleasure. I- I-I go because for reasons f-from the g-government you g-guys can-n-not hear about."

She looked shaken up, but let out a sigh of relief as

the bell rung. She screamed, "Have your mom look over the paper and sign it," while everybody took their bags and rushed out of class for lunch, but I lingered for a bit, watching her.

Ms. B glanced up as everyone followed the exit and took out a silver necklace from underneath her dark purple shirt. It was a chain that appeared to have a locket attached to it. She opened it and a single tear slipped from her eye. Though she quickly wiped it when she realized I was still in the room. She turned her back on me so that I couldn't see her anymore.

I threw my book bag over my back and walked out of the classroom towards the dining hall for lunch, walking in a daze, and wondering why Ms. B was sad, and acting so strangely.

~

The next few days passed in a blur. Ms. B was getting rather excited for the upcoming trip, which she would be attending, surprisingly, and all she could talk about was the trip and everything to do with the trip, and the trip, and the trip, and the trip.

Most of the girls in my class, too, were growing anxious and more excited for it. All the seniors were gossiping about what they would see and find. One of the stories I heard was that the males have five arms and no legs, and their eyes are not a natural color, but rather have a vibrant red hue to them. I didn't believe it of course, because that was ridiculous, like that old story about Santa Clause.

When the final day before the trip arrive, I will admit that I was getting nervous for it, but it was a good kind of nervous, and I wasn't the only one. Mary, the bossy girl with the straight brown hair, was pacing the room, and talking to calm herself down. But Ms. B was in good spirits.

"Well, class, I have a few reminders about the trip. Today is November seventeenth, which means tomorrow, November eighteenth, is the day we leave. Remember that you must be here on time tomorrow, so you do not miss the train. We had that problem last year, so please be careful about that."

The rest of the speech she was giving was all about the people who miss behaved in the pass while at the facility, probably just to scare us. It was boring, but I didn't put my head down, and so I sat and waited. When she finished she put on a video for us to watch, dimming the lights, which happened to be another speech. This, too, was boring.

" I am so happy you girls are going this week," the head of First Division began. " You are the third set of seniors to be trying this new system out, so make me proud." She smiled with falseness.

"This week you are embarking on such a journey that will change your lives forever. You are going to learn that we, as females, are superior to the males. You are going to learn what disgusting creatures they are. You are going to learn why the Women had this revolution many years ago.

"I cannot express to you all how vulnerable you all really are going to the facility, but I have faith in Christy Pepper that you will chose to believe in what is *right*.

"I bid good luck to the whole of you." The head of First Division smiled her last fake smiles, and disappeared off screen. Then she reappeared saying, "Thank you," and the video ended. The video went back to the home screen of the head of First Division wearing her signature color, yellow, in a long, sweeping dress. She was prancing around a garden of daffodils, laughing, while her skin on her pale face stretched.

The lights came on again, and we actually started working too, but Ms. B never stopped talking to us. Before class was dismissed, Ms. B handed out a dark, amber envelope with our names inscribed on them, slipped it into my pocket, and was left to wandering around, thinking about the trip tomorrow.

~

The rest of my day was easy. I went to lunch, sat with my best friend Lyanna, and then went to study hall where I didn't study, but sat the whole time thinking. After school dismissed completely, I walked home and was surprised to see that my mom was back so soon, because usually she didn't get off work until five.

"How was your day at school?" she asked, as I was walking through the door. I was greeted by smells of potatoes and meat wafting through the entryway, and by my mother in an old apron atop of her black skirt and shirt with a cutting knife in her hand.

27

"Fine." I sat my book bag on the square table in the kitchen and watched my mom stand mixing the potatoes. "We had to listen to the head of First Division today, which was boring, and consuming the time I have left in this life, and-"

"God, that women is so stupid!" my mom shouted, flinging bits of potatoes around in the kitchen. My mouth dropped; it was unlawful for a citizen to disrespect the government, but even more inappropriate for her to belittle Christy Labelle.

My mom corrected herself though, as quickly as the words slipped her tongue. "What I meant to say was that that woman isn't as bright as we all think she is, but thank goodness we have her as the head…" and then she rambled on and on about how great Christy LaBelle, the head of First Division, is.

She didn't say much after that, but continued solely on finishing diner. Her brown eyes looked embarrassed and upset and confused and her thin body was trembling very fast. I left the kitchen as soon as she looked well enough for me to leave; she didn't look like she wanted to converse with me. And I had to start packing for tomorrow's trip.

I remember the envelope I got earlier and pulled it out of my pocket. I was glad I remembered it, because the first thing it said on the letter was packing.

incognito

I am so very pleased to notify that you, Samantha Yards, will be going on the trip to Incognito. In this letter you will find the items you need to pack while away, and several instructions I feel as if you should know too.

Thanks,

Christy Pepper

Christy Pepper, Head of First Division, Subdivision 5

Packing:

- Ten pairs of jeans
- Ten shirts, white
- No toiletries
- No books, movies, games, etc.

Packing shouldn't have been hard, but it was. The list

required all the girls to bring ten pairs of long jeans to Incognito, as well as ten different shirts. The shirts had to be long and had to be able to cover everything, and couldn't be the colors you wanted, it had to be in white. And then I couldn't bring any books with me to read, or music, or electronics that could somehow get lost or taken by the males. But even when I didn't have the extra items, I still had trouble fitting it all into the suitcase.

The only thing I could thank Incognito for was that I didn't have to bring a toothbrush or pillow because they would be providing that for me. And it was a good thing too, that they were doing that for us, because the people the boys would probably give our essential items unwanted germs that could infect us; I didn't want that.

I grasped the handle of my black suitcase, which was more rounded than square because of all the clothes comprised in it- and rolled it to the front of the hall at the door.

"I forgot all about the trip. It is tomorrow, isn't?" My mom came out and set her hand on my shoulder. I nodded, and then murmured, "Dinner," in my ear.

I dawdled through the living room into the kitchen, smelling the steak and potatoes, but I didn't feel like eating. But I grabbed a plate anyway, and sat down with my mom. We grabbed each other's hands and mom said the prayer.

"Bless this food, Bless Sam's trip tomorrow, and Bless everybody in the world, Amen." Her soft voice ended with a hum, and she squeezed my hand.

"Amen," I repeated. By the end of the prayer, the smells were getting to me, and we sat in silence for a few minutes, eating.

"Mom, can I ask you a question?" I requested, shoving some potatoes in my mouth.

"You can ask another, if that is what you mean," she stated with a smile, shoving more food into her mouth.

"I was just wondering, what happens when a mother has a child ...and it is a male?"

Her eyes grew big, and she swallowed. It looked like I had sucked the life out of her, and she delayed answering the question. After a few moments she looked up to me.

"I'd rather not talk about that. It is a really tough subject, honey. Why don't you just eat, yes?" She put more food back into her mouth.

I didn't press any further about the issue, but something was up; I could feel it. I finished dinner in silence after that, and cleaned up silently. My mom left the room to take a shower, and when everything was done, I did too. But as I passed her room to my bathroom, I heard crying.

I peered through her cracked door and saw my mom's back. Her head was down, but I could hear her silently crying. I knocked on it, slightly, and she turned, shoving something under the bed.

"I'm going to go take a walk, okay." She stood up and started heading towards me. "Do you need anything?"

"No," I whispered. I walked to my bathroom and stared through the blinds waiting to see my mom outside. Once I saw her walking on the sidewalk, I ran to her room, and looked underneath the bed.

Shock filtered all through out my body. I couldn't believe what I was looking at, or what I saw was even right. I was holding an old photograph with a baby in it.

The baby was a normal looking baby; wrinkly and happy with large, brown eyes. The only problem was the date of birth of the baby. I was born in the year 2117, but the date on the picture says 2116. That couldn't be right, and pictures never print out the wrong date. This could only mean one thing; this baby wasn't me.

Then who was it?

I waited on the couch with the picture until my mom got home. And she got home, she wasn't too happy when she saw what I was holding.

"Where did you get that?" she asked

"Who is this, mom?" I demanded. I waited, but she didn't say anything. So I asked again. "WHO IS THIS?"

"That was my son," she admitted. She hung her head in shame, avoiding me.

"You mean- as in- you had a male?" I was stunned. She was breaking so many laws having that picture in the house.

"Yes, " she breathed. Tears started rolling down her cheeks. "Maybe you'll understand that ten years, if you have one, and you have to give him up."

She looked at the picture, and then looked back to me. "I didn't want to say anything to you tonight. But you cannot tell a soul about this picture."

"Where did he go?"

"I honestly don't know." She hung her head down again. "I got to hold him for a minute, and luckily the doctors who helped me give birth were a little lenient about the rules. And your aunt took the picture, but nobody knows except her and me, and now you."

I took a second to take it all in. While I did that my mom came and sat back down with me, and stared at the curtain. She was breaking so many rules by just having that picture, let alone that she is discussing it now.

"Did you have a name for him?" I asked her, pointing at the picture. She turned it back over so that the baby was facing us.

"No, not right away. I didn't know it was a boy inside me, so I picked the name right on the spot so I picked Sam," she answered. That caught me off guard.

"Is that how you named me?" It was important to me to keep asking questions. I needed to know. I think there was a part inside of me that always knew, because my mom never spoke about anything like this.

"Yes," she confessed. "The name on your birth certificate says Samantha because I had to show that it a

34

girls name, and not a boys. But I have always called you Sam." She looked at me, smiled, and added, "It's sort of always worked too, you know."

I stood up the couch and hugged her. I had had enough for one night. I was learning so much about a person I thought I knew, but I kind of liked this side of her. It was sort of rebellious, and daring, and very unlike her.

When I finally got into my bed, the clock beside it was ticking closer and closer to midnight. I didn't know we had talked for that long, so I turned over and stared as the numbers ticked by letting my thoughts drift off.

CHAPTER 3.

I woke the next morning having slept only an hour; my thoughts about what Incognito was going to look like filled my head with images that were probably unlikely to happen. But by the time I had pulled my long jeans on and jacket, I didn't have much time to waste.

When I came out of my room, my mom was waiting for me at the table; she had cooked breakfast, and had it sprawled out all over, ranging from eggs to pastries to toast and to cereal. I sat down and gathered a little but eagerly wished that I were actually hungry, but the butterflies in my stomach fluttered hard, and pounded my whole front side, so I nibbled.

"I don't know how the food is at Incognito," she stated sarcastically. She was eating herself, but a much bigger portion than I.

36

"I'm not that hungry," I told her. I finished the little bit of pastry I had left on my plate and checked the clock. I needed to be at school in fifteen minutes.

"You ready?" my mom asked. She got up from the table and grabbed her car keys, urging me to follow her. And soon I was.

And soon we were in the car passing all the other rectangular houses down my street; passing the buildings that divided the neighborhood from the actual city; passing little girls with their moms frolicking on the sidewalk.

And then we pulled up to my secondary school. I said my goodbyes to my mom, pulled my heavy suitcase out, and eventually found all the seniors in my classroom with their heavy suitcases that looked similar to mine.

My friend Lyanna was already in the room with her suitcase, but from the looks of it, it looked bigger than her.

"Ready for the trip?" I asked her, but I don't know why I bothered asking her; she looked ready. She hadn't made the effort to change into her clothes; she still had her pajamas on.

"I was born ready," she laughed, "My momma even said so."

I laughed at her, I laughed with her, and I laughed at her luggage that was twice the size she was because she was a small Asian girl. Her tan skin was much darker then most of the girls at the school, and the same thing goes with her hair; it was very straight, and very black.

Even though she was my friend, we just stood there like we didn't know each other, in silence, not talking, staring off into who knows where.

Standing didn't last for long though, because as soon as we had begun getting comfortable, Ms. B came in, her face exploding with happiness.

"Everybody line up, please," she ordered. "Shortest to tallest, too," she added. Lyanna and I looked at each other, and walked straight to the front. I was just a little taller to her four foot seven.

"Now we are just waiting for the bell to ring," she said. She held her hands in front of her body, anxiously waiting.

When the bell finally rung, we filed out of the school until we reached the street. The train station was only across the street from our school, so we crossed and then we were there.

The train was dark blue, and smoke billowed from the horn on top. The conductor was already in her seat pushing buttons while another girl in a blue outfit was at a door on the side of the train screaming, "Come this way, yeah that 's right, leave your luggage on the ground, we will take care of it -yep- keep comin'."

We all followed her orders, and filed in. Down the train there were many compartments with all sorts of neat seats, but the section that we were sitting in were of rows and rows of seats.

"Lets sit here," Lyanna whispered, pointing to the seats in the front near the doors. As we did, we saw all the other girls file in the back where they were away from us. Ms. B took her time meandering through the doorway, sitting in the seats that were directly in front of us, the ones we couldn't sit in.

"I hope this is a short train ride," Lyanna muttered, but I wasn't sure if she was just talking to herself.

There was a screeching noise above us on the ceiling of a train, and a high-pitched woman's voice came on. "Okay girls, we are about to depart. Please stay in your seats and put your seat belts on. Thank you."

I pulled the seatbelt over my chest and clipped it in. About fifty more clipping sounds could be heard rebounding off the interior of the train, and then the train rumbled to life. Objects started passing us through the small square window in the train, and we were off. My heart skipped a few beats.

"I wonder who were going to get?" I thought aloud, and turned my head so that I was facing Lyanna now.

"I don't know, nor do I care," she responded, leaning the train seat back so that she was reclining.

"But think about it, what if they are dangerous or-"

"You are so annoying, did you know? All you want to do is talk, and talk, and talk, and right now I don't have the energy right now to talk, so if you excuse me, I am going to sleep. Wake me when we stop for food, and leave me be," she said playfully, and angrily. I shrugged; this was how she always was.

I turned back and looked out the window and watched all the buildings pass by. Soon we had left the city, and the buildings had morphed into tall trees and farmhouses in the country, stretching beyond miles of unused masses of land.

I don't know how long it had been, but I just sat there and stared through the glass. My ears perked up when I heard a ringing sound, and a hushed voice.

"I'm on my way right now," the voice squeaked. It was Ms. B on the phone.

I tugged on Lyanna's pajama shirt. As I did, her eyes barely opened, but then she shut again; she waved her hand as if trying to tell me to stop it, but I wasn't going to stop, so I tugged her shirt once more.

"Wha-"

I put my fingers to my lips, and pointed to Ms. B in front of us. Then I mouthed the word 'listen'.

"... Well I don't know how much further its going to be... Yes, I know... Jeremy, tell your brother I said I loved him, and I'll see him very, very soon." Ms. B's voice was still in a hushed whisper, and I heard the phone click.

The seat she was sitting in pushed back a little bit as she rested her body back down. Lyanna and I both jumped back , so that our backs were plastered against our seats. We didn't say anything for a moment about what we had just heard, but instead kept our mouths close and eyes focused on the blue sky.

41

"Don't you realize what we just heard?" I asked in a quiet voice to Lyanna. She didn't look as shaken up as I was.

"Ms. B was just talking on the phone, what's the big deal?"

"She wasn't just talking on the phone! She said Jeremy, and brother. I think she was talking to a *boy*?"

"Don't you dare say that! She must have mixed up the words, don't you think? Look, It's against the rules for her to do that, so I don't think she's breaking them. And if this is what I am going to be waken up to again, don't do it…." she rambled on, and then settled back down until she was comfortably asleep. The

Ms. B wasn't sitting there talking to a girl; girls don't have boy names; people in the society do not mix up the word sister for brother, because brothers don't exist.

There was a crack between the two seats in front where Ms. B was sitting, so I kept my eyes focused on the point on it. After her phone call, she checked her phone two more times, and then she asked the conductor how much longer until we would arrive. But then she took that locket out again, and this time I got a better look into it.

I couldn't see much through the crack, but this time I saw that the locket had two faces in them, and they were bother boys. They looked different though, because the baby picture I saw last night looked like me when I was a baby, and these two faces didn't look like girls at all; the hair was short, and their faces were more hard than soft. It was weird.

I didn't have much time to process that because the lady with the high-pitched voice came back on again on the ceiling. "We will be arriving in a few minutes, please be ready with all your belongings you have with you one the train."

I nudged Lyanna again, and eyed the restroom in the back where she could change. By the time she got out, the train was slowing down, the door was opening, and Ms. B was standing up calling all of us.

"Follow me, girls. We will have to walk for a minute because the train does not have access inside the facility. Lets go"

Lyanna, who finally dressed in proper attire, and I were out first, besides Ms. B. The rest of the girls came out a second after us, and there were two women unloading our suitcases onto the ground.

Once all the suitcases and girls were out of the train, it slowly gathered some speed and disappeared into the horizon. We were now in the middle of nowhere facing a large gate, with two guards at the front.

"I need to see some I.D. mam," one of the ladies said.

"She's cleared, Carson, its just Ellison. She is a monthly visitor," the other guard answered. She then faced Ellison and asked her, "How are you doing today?"

"Good, good. I'm just getting these senior girls out here to do their report," she answered proudly, yet there was hesitation in her voice.

"Okay then," Carson spat. Her nose scrunched up a bit as if she was going to sneeze, but it didn't come, and grabbed her walkie-talkie, pulled it to her mouth, and said, "Okay, Mal, open up the gates please." And as soon as the last word poured out of her mouth, the gates started opening.

All of the seniors were pushing past each other trying to get a look around; I will admit, it was a beautiful site to see. Besides the ruddy gate that enclosed the space, everything was open. The field extended far beyond what I could see, and the facility was painted to blend in with it. The lower part of the building was a soft green that matched the grass, and the top of it was white with a tint of blue.

Down the path was a white bus that looked like a really big golf cart, waiting for us to come to it, so I started walking faster.

"This is a little better than I expected," I said to Lyanna who wasn't listening to me; she was turning her head every two seconds to see the place.

Girls ahead of us had reached the bus and loaded their suitcase onto it when I realized Lyanna and I were the only ones left who hadn't gotten on the bus, so we started walking faster.

"Hurry up, girls," Ms. B called. She was stretched out in the front seat next to the driver.

After we finally made it and were settled, the bus started driving us down the path to go to the facility, but then took a wild turn onto a path that didn't even look like a path at all.

The driver yelled, "Don't worry, we're not entering the front of the building, we're coming in from the ground floor," too help calm down a few of the people who gasped, but for all I knew, we weren't at the facility anymore, we were in the forest.

The way the driver was taking us was crazy to; we never took any ninety-degree angle turns, we took curved and unexpected turns; we didn't follow a path, the driver made up the path. We had made it so deep into the forest that the only thing that could be seen was all the trees and plants, but soon the trees disappeared and we broke through to be facing what looked like a garage.

As the driver pulled up to the garage, it opened, and she told us to get out. And when we all did, she said that someone would bring our luggage up to our rooms.

I turned my head to get a better look at where I was, and saw a woman standing behind me.

"Welcome, welcome, seniors," she called out to all of us. She was easily six feet tall, and was a very tiny woman.

"My name is Allison Doe, and I just wanted to clear a few things up before we begin the tour. First you need to know that you cannot leave this campus until your stay is over, but I doubt any of you would try; its very hard to get pass our guards.

"Secondly, you need to know that the creatures in this building are not to be trusted. People get killed because of the information they give out. I cannot begin to express to you how important it is to listen to the rules, because I would hate to see one of you get hurt." She paused, and then looked back at us. "Now, let's go inside. "

There were two large, double doors next to the garage where she took us into it, which was followed by a single, long hall. The walls were white, which made it seem like it would never end, and every ten feet or so, there were devices on the ceilings. I wasn't sure, but they looked like cameras, or lasers, or both.

When we finally reached the end, there was a door that looked like it was made out of concrete. Ms. Doe took a key out and unlocked it, and everybody's jaw dropped.

The inside was unlike anything I'd, or anybody in the room, had seen before. It was a large, circular room probably three stories high that were painted the same color: gray. Brown doors lined most of the bottom of the room, but I also saw other colors, like green and yellow and red, but if I had had time to count them, I don't think I could count all of them. Then Ms. Doe rambled on about which rooms we were not supposed to go in, which were all the colors accept brown, and she directed us through one of the brown doors.

"If you could all take your seats at the tables, we will call you and take you to find the boy you will be observing." Ms. Doe stepped up to the front of the dining hall, and took out a list where she started reading the girls names aloud.

"Amy Armstrong," Ms. Doe called," You will be observing B7."

I turned my head towards the only place I saw a door, and instead of the boy I thought I would get to see, I saw yet another woman come out, who I guessed would escort Amy to B7.

I stopped listening for a while, because I would be the last person to be called; my name was Samantha Yards, so I was pretty sure I would be last. I heard Lyanna's name get called, and she would be observing O2, and then she was escorted out, looking very awkward.

It dawned on me that I was the last person in the room, except for Ms. Doe, and she too, made this discovery and looked at me and said, "Samantha, you will be observing E5. Why don't you follow me."

Ms. Doe waited for me at the door, and led me through a series of other doors that I couldn't keep up with, where we ended up outside. It was a strange, looking courtyard, with several basketball courts in it, and many small people playing in the distance. Ms. Doe reached into her dress pocket, took out a whistle, and blew it, and all the small people in the distance lined up where they were.

"I need E5," Ms. Doe called. I saw one of the boys come foreword and walk towards us. I hadn't noticed before, but I was suddenly growing anxious; my palms were sweating and my legs were growing weak. I had never seen a boy up close.

"Samantha, this is E5. E5, this is Samantha. Meet back up in the dining hall in an hour for further instructions."

CHAPTER 4.

The boy was different than I expected. He was
normal looking, except he wasn't a girl; his figure was not
curvy, but straight, and everything about him was larger
than what I was used to seeing; his hands, his feet, his face,
they were tougher looking.

"Is this how you plan on observing me, or do you
plan on doing any work?" he smirked. His voice caught me
off guard; it was really low and rough. Then he scowled,
turned, and started walking away from me.

"Hey," I screamed, " don't walk away. Slow down!" I
was jogging to keep up with him, surprisingly out of
breath.

"I don't have time for this," he barked, rolling his
eyes. He stopped so I could catch my breath.

"Well you need to make time," I retorted in between breaths.

"You *girls* are ignorant and careless; if *you* don't give a flip about me, then I don't give a flip about *you,*" he paused, making himself clear that he didn't want me to talk.

I didn't say anything back. I was too shocked that he was yelling at me, and I felt guilty, which was even more surprising. He started walking back to the pen of guys playing basketball, and joined back in.

There was a bench that was positioned on the outskirts of the court, so I sat there watching them, specifically E5. I also gave some thinking into what E5 had said to me, which started to send mix signals through my body. Why was I feeling sorry for him? After all, he is a creature in the eyes of the government.

But my mind kept arguing.

He must be manipulating you somehow, I said.

No, he's acting normal somehow, so he cannot be, I retorted back.

You cannot feel sorry for him! He should feel sorry for himself.

I felt like I had my good cochins on one shoulder, and the bad cochins on the other, telling me what to think.

I tried to get my mind off of my confusing thoughts and watched how easy it was for E5 to simply dunk the ball into the basket. His muscles were much bigger than mine- or should I say girls in general? - and bulged right out of the skin, making funny lumps in his arms and legs. Rarely are girls ever seen with this kind of strength, or wearing items of clothing to show it off, because that shows signs of weakness in my society, and girls cannot appear to be weak.

I pulled my eyes off him and looked away completely; I didn't feel like trying to watch him right now, especially because he was making me angry, and making myself angry with myself. I started to get a headache.

The rest of the hour was short-lived by a fight that broke out (which I didn't watch), and a few officers coming and using some kind of weapon that made them drop to the ground like flies.

When the bell that signaled lunch rang, E5, unwillingly, dragged himself over to me so we could go eat, but I could tell he didn't want to be near me. He walked a few feet away from me, and stayed silent the whole walk up to the facility.

The face of the building I was looking at looked completely different from where I had come out before. Large, open windows decorated most of the back of it, so I headed to the nearest door to me.

"Unless you want to head down to the cells and punishment rooms, I would follow me, " he sneered. I felt bothered by what he said, because it wasn't even meant to be mean, but the way he said it was rude.

So I followed him and kept my distance. He picked the only other door that was on the south side of the wall, and as soon as we opened it, we had found where we needed to be.

The dining hall where I had been in earlier now was filled with smells of different types of meat and cheeses. The tables were now filled with plates of sandwiches, and the chairs with girls and boys; it was an interesting sight to see; never in my life had I seen girls and boys sitting together at tables.

In the distance I found Lyanna sitting with a very skinny boy; the boy looked so infatuated with her, but it was obvious looking at her face that she could be doing something else now, like sleeping, at home than being here.

Mary, the girl with the straight brown hair, was sitting with her back to the boy she was sitting with, talking to some of her friends. Mary look disgusted, and while most of the boys and women in the facility might think she just didn't like the food, she despised the boy. I even saw Rebecca, but it didn't look like being here in the facility changed how much she talked, because she just sat there staring at the boy she was partnered up with.

A sensation of gratitude filled me, because even though I was bickering with my partner, at least I talked to him, and could get actual feedback from him to write in my essay.

It didn't take long to grab lunch. The line was quick, and there weren't too many options to choose from, so most of us were eating the same thing anyway. There was only one vacant table left in the dining hall, so E5 and I walked over there.

The first few minutes were awkward, for me at least; they were very silent. But I broke the silence.

"Do you have a name?" I blurted out.

"E5."

"Don't you have a regular name?"

"No."

"I don't mean to be rude," I apologized. "The life here is just too different from my life at home."

He actually cracked a smile.

I was getting somewhere.

"Sorry for my interruption," Ms. Doe chimed in, "but I wanted to let you guys no what the schedule is for the rest of the day." She grabbed a piece of paper that she pulled out, scanned over, and read aloud.

"Your partner will now walk you around Incognito, explaining the rules. You must stay together, and there will be punishment if you don't. Seniors," Ms. Doe paused and looked around at all of the girls, "remember that it is your duty to be observing the boy life, so no socializing with your girlfriends."

She gave the evil eye to Mary and her friends, and left it at that, disappearing with a few of the guards. There was a rush of chairs scratching the floor, and then I looked at E5 and asked, "Where to?"

"Lets start at the very top of Incognito, and work our way down."

Unlike the rest of the girls with their partners who dispersed all throughout the ground floor, we headed to the top floor. There was a heavy door in the front of the dining hall, which was the staircase that we used; I had to climb five flights of stairs.

I groaned, and trailed about ten steps behind E5, because I didn't want to get too close to him. He liked his space, so I respected that, because I really needed him to cooperate with me. And then ten thousand, long, heavy, flat, hard steps later, we were up. I had to stop and catch my breath, but he looked ready.

"We never have access around Incognito like this," he explained, walking forward into the depths of a very wide hallway. The floor was dark purple, while the walls gleamed white. This wide hallway had pictures of women along the walls, and three doors.

"This is Ms. Doe's office," he said, pointing to the left of us. Her picture hung on the door, her sallow face covered in makeup. "Were not actually allowed on this floor, but, since they said…" he let his sentence hung for a minute, but as he began to explain the second door, we heard a voice. We crept a little closer to it, putting our ears slightly on it.

".. and that would be breaking every rule," a girls voice rang. It was Ms. B's, and then is dawned on me that I hadn't seen her in a few hours. Why was she here? Where had she gone? The door was slightly ajar, and another voice, male, spoke.

"Mom, I want to do it. Michael to, and a few others I'm sure would agree, " The male voice whispered angry. It was lower than E5's.

"Jeremy, it's the safest place to talk freely without someone making the wrong assumption, its dangerous out there."

There was a noise, and the door started opening. We both jumped high into the sky, and ran into the nearest room, holding our breath. I crouched down and E5 hid behind a bookcase, but the door was still wide open. The first set of footsteps passed by, and then a minute later, another set of footsteps passed by, but these were heavier footsteps than before. Ms. B and Jeremy were gone.

I straightened myself back up a little bit, relieved. My heart thudded against my chest, and looked back at E5 and asked him, "Do you know who Jeremy is?"

"I don't think you get it. All the people here in Incognito have names like E5, or U9, or something like that. He probably has a name in that similar fashion, but that woman renamed him."

After a minute of thought, I realized that Jeremy was the same person who spoke to Ms. B earlier, so he must be her son. And then Michael must be the other boy of hers.

I stepped forewords ready to leave, and hit something hard on the wall, which turned the light on. E5 and I both gasped, hundreds of pictures of Ms. Doe and posters lined the inside of her office. But not only had I turned the light on, I knocked over some papers.

"Quickly grab them. I don't want her to know we were up here," I said to E5, and then right after that, the thud of the heavy door from the stairs settled back into place, and footsteps headed our way.

"Hide!"

I dashed across the room, which was still lit, behind the desk that Ms. Doe had, and crawled underneath it. There was the tiniest crack in the top corner of the little space I was in, so I peered through it. E5 was glued to the wall behind the bookshelf, and a shadow appeared near the doorway.

"Check the area please. 1 just came through the staircase which makes me wonder…" Ms. Doe's ordered. Two people dressed in blue passed by, while it looked like Ms. Doe had stopped in front of her room.

" I thought I had turned this light off."

I held my breath because she wandered right on in, and stopped midway.

Please don't let her see me; please don't let her see me, I prayed.

Her feet took a small step, and then the light clicked off. Then she walked out of the room and shut the door where I could hear a muffled form of her voice. "Did you find anything Carson and Mal?"

While I couldn't hear what the guards from the front gate earlier had said, I sat in the room using what little light I had to look at the papers I had knocked down. A few of them looked like floor plans, with squares and boxes and little numbers filling the whole space. The last paper was a letter, so I stuck both of them in my pocket. Several yellow balloons fell, too, but I stuck them back on her desk. I tilted my head towards the crack and didn't hear anymore voices, or footsteps.

"I think were good," I whispered to E5.

I slowly climbed out from under the desk, found the wall, and used it to guide me to the door. I opened it, but before leaving the room, I stuck my head out to see if anyone was out there.

"Clear," I motioned. We swiftly marched through the door, E5 shutting it silently.

"I think it's better, for the both of us, to see the other levels. This has been… interesting," E5 suggested. So, I did what he said. We ventured through the staircases and found the fourth floor, the floor beneath the top level, and only found where I would be staying. He somehow knew which room I was in, and then briefly walked me around the floor.

The third level was the most interesting by far. It contained all the rooms where the boys slept. I know it shouldn't have excited me, but this was territory I shouldn't have access to.

After looking at several of the rooms, I began to notice that all the rooms looked the same; tiny and light brown. There was only enough room to have a small bed situated in the corner and a chest of draws.

"And this," E5 said, turning the door handle, "is my room."

He sounded really happy about his, but I didn't see why. It was tiny and the walls were painted light brown; his bed was in the corner, but there was a door on the ceiling. I looked up at it; his eyes met mine.

"That is not just any door, before you make assumptions. It connects to the ventilation system throughout most of Incognito," he whispered. He hopped onto the bed, wacked the wall, and pulled down the string that fell. When he did that, the door on the ceiling fell.

He started bouncing on the bed, when a crash came from outside of his room. Screams could be heard trailing down the hallway; he shot off the bed, fear wiping his face.

"WHAT HAVE YOU DONE?" Ms. Doe screamed. I went outside thinking she was talking to E5, and me, but she wasn't. She had a whip in her hand, and was striking a muscular, skinny boy who was crouched on the floor, bleeding.

"I HAVENT DONE NOTHING, LADY," the boy screamed back. Anger filled his voice while tears washed his face.

"Lets go," E5 whispered. He gently put his hands on my back and pushed me quietly down the hall. I was surprised because he actually made physical contact with me, but the fact that Ms. Doe was beating a boy. The screams from his voice still echoed through my ears as we made our way down to the lower levels of Incognito.

CHAPTER 5.

E5 didn't want me around the guy who was getting beaten, so we eventually made our way back outside, wandering around. E5 was very talkative and spoke about every subject he knew, and the ones that I didn't know.

Incognito, as he said to me earlier, had pulled out the older and younger guys and had moved them to a neighboring facility to house them while we were here. It hadn't dawned on me yet that boys aged too, but it was hard for me to think about; I hadn't seen one before so I wouldn't know what to look for expect maybe something out of the ordinary. Besides that, it seemed like the only reason why the older and younger boys were missing was for our safety, but I began to wonder if it was because of Ms. Doe, whom I'm sure made arrangements for it right away.

The beatings the boy received earlier was actually a toned down punishment from what they normally got too. E5 even had scars to show me, which he willingly did, on the back of his neck and arms, and all I could think was how painful it must've been when it happened. I hadn't even broken a bone in my body, let alone get a paper cut.

While walking around outside, I noticed that E5's physical appearance reminded me of myself. He had dark brown hair that hung above his green and blue eyes kind of like me, and his nose was more rounded than pointed, just like mine.

"Can I call you by a different name?" I asked. "I just don't feel like E5 is an actual name."

All I got for an answer was a blank stare. I continued.

"I mean, if you like E5 then by all means..." I stated, repeating the same sentences over and over again. Eventually, he cracked, and gave answered me.

"If it'll make you stop talking, sure," he retorted. "I don't know what you'll call me-"

"I'll call you Samuel, its settled."

"But isn't your name Samantha? Its kind of close-"

"It'll work," I argued back.

And from then on, I called him Samuel. It was challenging not to call him by Samuel in front of the other people, but I made sure to be mindful of the adults and other girls because I didn't want us getting into trouble. I would have been scowled at about giving him a name, but worse, Samuel would have probably been beaten.

~

When dinner finally rolled around, the boys grabbed their plates of food, and disappeared. I didn't see what was on their plates, but it didn't look appetizing at all. Then there was a scuffling sound coming from the dining hall food line, and clanking of dishes. It appeared that the dinner the boys had was getting replaced; I assumed it was probably better food.

I assumed correctly. The food down the line looked very colorful: strawberries, blueberries, apples, raspberries, green beans, corn. After the colorful food was a butt-load of Italian dishes, steaming hot, and emitting a wonderful smell that broadcasted throughout the dining hall. I

grabbed a little of everything, and sat down with Lyanna;
she looked exhausted; however, she had a lot to say.

"… He's so weird. I understand now why they are
separated from society. I only know what the government
says, but they are absolutely right. He's a monster. He is so
rude, and ugly and…" Lyanna took a bite of her lasagna
and went straight back into conversation. I just listened –
even though I didn't like anything that she was saying- and
nodded my head at the appropriate places, until Ms. Doe
interrupted her.

"Hello- can I get everybody's attention- thank you.
Before you all leave, your teacher is going to say a few
words. Ms. B?" Ms. Doe asked, looking around. A lot of
the girl's heads turned to, to the left, to the right, to the
side. She wasn't in the room.   "Ms. B
are you in here?" Ms. Doe asked again. But for the second
time, there was no response. A clattering of the doors to
the dining hall made our heads jerk towards it to see an
awfully distressed Ms. B come racing in.

"Sorry, I'm coming, I'm coming," Ms. B called. Her
curly blonde hair blew past her face as she ran across the
large room. She bumped into a few of the tables along the
way, and when she got closer, dirt covered her face, and

she was out of breath.

"Sorry," she said, in and out of breathes. "I was talking to one of the guards when I realized what time it was." Ms. B turned towards all of us, straightened out her clothes, and then began again.

"Well, I hope your first day was successful. Tomorrow begins your observations, so you will need a pencil and some paper to write on. Breakfast will start at seven thirty, and go through nine. You should also remember that your time with your partner starts at eight thirty, and will end at five tomorrow evening. And don't," she emphasized, "Go wandering around the building tonight. You will be sent home, and be suspended from school. Do you understand?"

We all nodded our heads vigorously and finished up eating. Then we were escorted up the treacherous walk up to the fourth level where all of our belongings were, and where we were sleeping. I already knew where my room was, thanks to Samuel, and was rooming with Lyanna.

This room was bigger than Samuels by a landslide, and brighter to. Not only were the walls bright blue, but there were two lamps in it too. Two beds, side by side, were on one of the walls with a light in between them while a door- I assume was the closet- filled the rest of the space up. On another wall, two dressers took the remaining space up, where it contained our suitcases.

It didn't take long to figure out we weren't tired, and that Lyanna wasn't finished talking. Something about her that is funny is that she isn't much of a talker, at all. In school she is as quiet as a predator stalking it's prey, but when you get her talking every now and then on a subject she feels strongly about, you will never hear the end of it. This night was one of those nights.

Most of what – actually, all of what- we talked about was still about Lyanna's boy she had been with, and how she didn't like him at all. When I got a chance to speak, I told her all about going on the top floor and having to hide from Ms. Doe, and what Ms. B had said, and about Ms. Doe whipping the boy. The only part I left out was giving Samuel a name, and about his secret door in his room because that probably wasn't the best thing to go ranting about.

She didn't seem shocked at all, or seemed to care. In fact, she gave the same response she did earlier on the train.

" Ms. Doe is just doing what she is supposed to. And

plus, If I could, I would have whipped my boy up and down-

"But she was so mean to him! You should have seen it!"

"I don't know if you have noticed, but Sam, you have the most absurd thoughts. You're probably just tired too. I know you didn't sleep at all last night, and Ms. B would know not to commit those crimes." She stared at me like I had made the whole thing up. Last week I may have believe her too, but not now.

"No. I think she's up to it something."

"Well, let me know when you find anything conclusive."

With in minutes she had fallen to sleep, and snored. It never ended.

I lay there for hours, staring at the ceiling, having another restless night. I drifted off eventually, and dreamt Ms. B was with Jeremy in public, and Ms. Doe was with her, talking and laughing like nothing was wrong.

~

The following morning, I made it down to breakfast just in time before it closed. First I woke up later, and nobody was on my floor anymore. Then I had to get dressed and find the dining hall, which wasn't hard, expect I forgot where the stairs were. But then I didn't have my notebook and pen to write, so I had to find my room again. All in all I had a very hectic-like morning.

When I finally did make it, Samuel was waiting for me in the dining hall. His brown hair was combed, neater than yesterday, and his eyes were alert.

"Well it took you long enough, did it not?" he smirked, smiling. His cheeks rose up high on his face, and then settled back down.

I shrugged, making a silly face, and then said, "Lets get to work, shall we?" I didn't hesitate. I needed to get my work done.

"Well you tell me, where should we start?" He looked very interested in whatever we were going to do, so we found a deserted room in the building. I asked him to tell me his story, and so he began.

~

Incognito

I don't know when my birthday is, but I know that I was born in 2116 and arrived that same year. I've always have lived here, at Incognito, and I have never been so far as the bordered gate that lines the property.

My first memory of this place was when I was probably three. One of the older boys had been messing around with each other, and had bumped into one of the women that come to check up on Incognito. The woman that this kid bumped into looked at him and screamed, "You monster!" right in his face.

She had a pistol with her, and brought it up to him, and shot him right then and there because he was thought of trying to go against the system. And at that time, I didn't know why the women would do that, or what had actually happened. Ms. Doe even explained it to me; she probably wasn't the best to do it though.

"E5," she had said, "it's for the best, and I want you to know that. The way this world operates are with the boys stationed here at the facilities, and he just didn't wasn't to listen to that."

That was the first time I saw someone shot at, and I

tried to forget, but I couldn't. Watching the guy fall and tumble to the ground was too much for me to see, so from that day forward, I listened and believed everything that women said.

When I got older, it got harder and harder for me to be around everybody. Watching the guards beat or whip the boys was always too much for me to handle, so I always acted like a good boy so that the women would have no reason to hurt me. I knew that if I tried to strike a women, I would probably be shot, and I wasn't about to risk my life, even if at some times it seemed like the best thing to do.

I can't remember when, but one day, at some point in my life, I realized that I needed to make the best of it. I started interacting again with the adults, and eventually, they started telling me things.

Not just anything, mind you, but secrets about the past that I wasn't aloud to say out-loud. It would happen at the most random times too, like when the guards had us marching outside in the rain, or during the ten minute break we had between building something for Ms. Doe. They said to me that the only reason why they told the rest of the boys my age, and me, so that we could eventually tell the younger boys to pass it on.

But even after I gained my ability to socialize again, I still resented the women. The accidents with the shootings and all the beatings and burnings and whippings made me hate them more, and I began to see it more the older I got. It was all making more since to me.

I sunk again, like a ship. Like the titanic did two hundred years ago. I had sunk so low, that there seemed to be nothing that could pull me out.

~

"Excuse me, but what's a titanic? I asked Samuel. It was one of the oddest words that I have ever heard.

Samuel looked at me very oddly, but then his eyes lit up. "That's right," he said. "You don't know about anything. All you need to know is that it was a ship over two hundred years ago that sunk because it hit an iceberg."

I nodded my head, and let him continue his story.

~

One day, after years and years of my hatred towards women, I think an angel sent from the lord saved me. And not in the name of Christy, the girl savior most of you girls worship, but the real lord. The real Lord that walked this earth thousands of years ago, and gave up his life

She was a woman herself, but different, very different from the ones I knew, and the ones I had met before.

She had a kind face, and eyes so brown and sweet that made me forget about all the women in the world, but her; I needed to focus on her. She approached me when I was outside cutting the grass, walking towards me very slowly as if she thought she would scare me off.

I stopped the lawn mower and looked her, rage soaring through my body.

"Are you okay?" she had asked me. She was so close to me that her shoulders were touching my arm.

"No," I had breathed. I didn't want to say too much incase I grew angry with her. But my gut was screaming at me; it told me she had all the answers I needed and that I needed to listen to her.

"Keep praying, my son. Just know that there are other women out there that don't approve of this way of treating you."

I had never heard an actual woman say that to me, or say anything like that. The worst part was that my mind was so badly trained, because I wanted to go report this kind woman about what she said, but I resisted. I listened to every word she breathed into the air.

"You need to remember to be good. Be good right now, be good tomorrow, and be good next year. There is going to come a time when this government is going to collapse, so until then, be good. When they collapse, you rise up. Do you promise me?" she asked.

I let my head roll up and down, but neglected to say anything. The kind woman put her small, girly hand on my hand, squeezed it tightly, and walked away.

That happened about a year ago, and it's all I ever think about. I keep wishing the woman would come back, but she doesn't, and hasn't. It doesn't mean I haven't forgotten her smile, or her laugh, because it's all that plays in my head when I have a bad day. The memory I have of her helps me through my bad memories, like the death of my friend X6.

It was never his death that bothered me, because he was old, and I learned that at the end of a persons life, it becomes way too hard for a body so frail to handle, so they pass on to another life. But he died at the feet of one of the guards, who could have cared less about him, and that's what bothered me.

His name was X6, and had been one of my friends since I could remember, and who had practically raised me; he was my equivalent of a mother.

He was always there for me, and was there when I needed to cool down from something I had seen, or from an order I was supposed to do. Even when I was in my most denial of stages, he was right there beside me, coaching me through anything I needed.

"Remember, E5," he had told me. "I have been in the facilities my whole life. I know what to do, and what not to do, and here, sir, is a fine example of you trying to get yourself banged up." He would give me that speech every time I came to him, upset about something, or just needed a healthy reminder of what I wasn't trying to do.

As he got older, his age was catching up to him, but he didn't want to acknowledge it. Sometimes I would purposefully try to slow him down so he could let his body rest, but he pushed back my suggestions. And then one day it eventually became too hard for him too walk; the pain in his legs were cutting so deep that one day I picked him up and would carry him on my shoulder.

He was thin, didn't eat much, and his hair had turned white and didn't exist on the top of his head anymore.

One day we were eating lunch, which wasn't much; it was the standard pile of brown mushy, gravy gush they gave us everyday. It was gross, but we still ate it.

X6 and I were sitting at the

When I first met you, I didn't like you. I had no reason why not to like you, but I didn't. But your attempts to try to befriend me reminded me of that kind woman. You were so nice to me; it caught be off guard. Then you add the fact that you reminded me of her with your brown hair and round nose that it made me think that I had seen it somewhere, which means it must have been that angel from last year.

CHAPTER 6.

I stared at him, my mouth to the floor.

I stared at him, my body in absolute shock.

I was angry with myself, for believing anything the older women said. I was sad for him and all the boys and men who had to go through this.

Why?

Then I felt arms around me, and not those of a women or girl- flimsy-like- but those of a boy. Samuel was comforting me, and I realized I was crying. We sat there forever like this, and it felt good.

"I'm so sorry," I whispered to Samuel.

Then it clicked.

He was born about a year before me. He had the same, brown hair as me, and the same changing, colored eyes. The women he described sounded a whole lot like mine.

He was my brother.

"If I told you something, your going to believe me, right?" I asked.

"Yes."

I hesitated for a minute. Who knew, what I might say could make him angry, but I let it go.

"You are my brother," I admitted. It felt right to say, and so wrong.

Samuel looked at me, his eyes searching me for something, but he believed me; I could sense it. I immediately felt guilty about the papers I took from Ms. Doe, so I told him I had something to show him, but we needed to be alone.

"I know just where we can go," he stated. He took me out from the dining hall and brought me outside to the grounds of Incognito, pointing to the forest. "We can go in there."

I didn't think we could go in there, but then I reminded myself I named Samuel, so I pushed back whatever fear I had and followed him. Instead of going straight to the forest, though, Samuel took me to the basement of Incognito, the punishment rooms.

"We can go through the pipes," he said, as he wounded us through the maze of the lowest level. He never showed me this level, but I understood why; it was nasty. The walls and rooms looked like they were caked in cobwebs and mold, and the cement floor was ice cold. I had to hold my breath.

I think we had found the end when Samuel stopped at the end of a deserted hallway. Several doors branched off, but he didn't chose to go through them, but rather chose to unwind the metal , circular top on the ground.

"If we climb down into here, we will be able to enter the forest," he informed me. He let me slide in first so that he could cover the top over the hole once he was in. I felt the bottom, and hopped down, almost slipping, while Samuel joined me.

"You don't happen to have a flashlight, do you?" I asked him. The only light I had was the light filtering through the six holes on the metal top.

"No, just stay close behind me and you'll be fine."

Samuel started stepping forward, so I stayed close behind like he said, even though I couldn't see anything. I could feel when we were turning left and right, and soon, a thousand rays of light peered in. The end of the pipe we were in was coming to an end.

"Is that the end?" I asked him.

"Yes," he answered, and soon I could hear the clanking of a ladder. "I'm going to go up first, okay?"

I nodded my head; though don't know why because he couldn't see me. The ladder clanked a little more, and the screeching sounds of metal filled my ears. Before I knew it, light entered the pipes and a pile of leaves fell into the pipes.

"Sorry," Samuel apologized. His face appeared over the sides of the tops and he reached his hand down to me. I grabbed it, and he helped me out of the pipe while I climbed the remaining steps.

The forest was nothing like I had ever seen before in my life. There were so many colors of red and orange flaking from the almost naked trees, and the sounds of them crunching was even better. Samuel screwed the top back and on, and stretched out and said, "Okay, where to?"

I honestly had know idea, because I just wanted a place where we could look at papers I had grabbed. I pointed to what I thought was north, and we started walking. When we came to a long enough, thick enough, log, we sat down and I retrieved the papers and showed them to him.

"I haven't read the letter, but I have looked at the floor plans. Do you have any idea what they mean?" I asked Samuel, handing them to him.

He examined them for a minute, shrugging, and said," I have know idea. What does the letter say?"

I unfolded the letter from my pocket and opened it. I set it in the middle of us so that we could both read it.

Dearest Allison,

I hope you are well and healthy, and the boys at Incognito are treating you right. By the way, how are things looking at Incognito? I have been thinking about this lately and have concluded that we need to change

Incognito. I have attached some floor plans to this letter, which I believe you should take a look at. It is what I think we ought to do to rearrange the whole layout of not just Incognito, but the rest of the facilities as well.

Again, I hope you are well, and that you look at them.

Thank you,

Christy Pepper

Ps. The process of demolishing everything will start in seven months.

"Let me see those plans again?" I asked Samuel. He passed me the papers and I sat on the ground, placing them in front of me. I didn't see how all three papers connected.

"Wait a minute, Samuel said, moving off the log next to me. He rearranged the papers into a different order, and looked at me. "It's steps. It looks like somebody is going to destroy Incognito."

I stared at the images, trying to understand them.

"What does this mean then?" I asked aloud. "So, in seven months-"

"That would be June," Samuel chimed in.

"- Christy Pepper is going to destroy this place?" I finished saying. I took the photos and examined them again, to make sure I was seeing it correctly, but I was.

"She can't do that," I murmured.

"Can't do what?" a voice asked. I turned my head around to see Ms. Doe, staring straight at us. I swiftly gathered the documents and stuffed them into my pockets, hoping she didn't see me.

"E5, I know you're aware of this, but you do know you're not aloud here, right?" she asked him sweetly. It was evident, though, that she didn't mean it, and then she smiled.

"Sorry, Ms. Doe, it was all my fault! I dragged E5 here, and-"

"Don't give me that sob story Samantha," Ms. Doe interrupted. "I am no fool!"

She marched her scrawny body over to us and grabbed Samuel by the ear, and me by the elbow, and dragged us away off the ground.

"You are into trouble," Ms. Doe snickered, but I couldn't tell whom she was talking to. My guess was that she meant it for the both of us though, judging by her physical contact to both Samuel and me.

"Wonder what type of punishment we should do for you?" she spoke aloud, still with her hands clamped down on us. She pulled us further down the pathway until Incognito broke through the trees, and released us.

Ms. Doe was behind us, poking us every now and then, as we walked across the field. In the distance, I could see Ms. B talking to someone, and I think it was her son. As soon as I had seen her, she whisked her son away, and she turned and saw me.

"There you are!" She called to us. She jogged the little distance that was separating her from our little group until she was with us.

"You will never believe where I found these two!" Ms. Doe belted. Ms. B's eyes widened, and she cocked her head.

"They were in the forest plotting something," Ms. Doe screamed. She jerked her hands in the air, and then said, "I don't know how you're going to punish-"

"Oh- You know- I'm so sorry, Allison. I meant for the guards to find them, but I sent them out to the forest to test how the guards were doing here," Ms. B suddenly said. I tried to keep my shock under the table so Ms. Doe wouldn't notice.

"But I'm super glad you found them, which can only mean you're doing an excellent job!" Ms. B said again. She patted Ms. Doe's shoulder saying, "Well, I must be off myself. I have to go organize that activity for you tomorrow."

Ms. Doe's face was growing redder and redder, while her lips thinned out onto a thin line on her face. As soon as Ms. B was out of the hearing range, Ms. Doe grabbed my elbow and yanked it towards her.

"I know what you were doing," she angrily whispered. "By the way, have any idea where my papers went from my desk?"

I looked at Ms. Doe and just stared blankly at her. "What papers?" I asked her, making my voice sound more innocent.

She scowled and stalked off, fuming form the ears. I

could hear the doors slam shut as she entered Incognito. I then faced Samuel and we burst out into a rage of laughing.

"Did you see her face as Ms. B said that?" I asked him, trying to control my laughter. I was having trouble keeping it contained, but Samuel was having more trouble.

"Yes," he laughed. "I did and it was so fun-" he couldn't finish the sentence because he fell into another laughing spell.

We walked back into Incognito, shocked that it was already dinnertime. He stood by the side of the dining hall as all the girls got their meals, and when we had all sat down, he and the rest of the boys got their mush of a meal, and left. I sat with Lyanna, while she choked down her meal.

"I-am-so-hungry," she said in between her mouthfuls of food. "He made me miss lunch today!"

I chuckled, and realized that I too, had not eaten lunch. My stomach growled and I inhaled my dinner almost instantly, and finished it before she did.

"Hey, do you know what activity we're doing tomorrow?" I asked Lyanna. I could tell she was confused.

"Nope," she stated. "Why?"

"Just asking," I answered. "Ms. B said she was planning some kind of activity but, I'm not sure what."

I shrugged my shoulders and finished the remaining bits of food on my plate, and by the time I finished, we were dismissed back up to our rooms. I ended up falling asleep in my clothes, and being late for breakfast the next morning.

~

Breakfast the next morning was as quick as it ever had been this week. I had slept through almost all of it, and was woken by Lyanna, barely getting down stairs to have a little cereal. When I had sat down at a seat, Ms. B was just beginning a speech.

".… Yes, I think this activity will be something you all enjoy. What you will be doing is a scavenger hunt with your partner throughout the grounds of Incognito. This is supposed to be a learning exercise to define the strengths of our bodies and minds. The instructions will be passed around," she finished. She stepped down from the podium she was standing at while several of the guards passed out the papers.

"YOU WILL HAVE FIVE MINUTES TO LOOK
THESE PAPERS OVER BEFORE YOU ARE
RELEASED TO FIND THE ITEMS," Ms. B added,
shouting over the noise of the dining hall.

Samuel came out of nowhere and sat beside me,
looking over the instructions we had been given. "This
should be really easy," he whispered in my ear. "All we
have to do is crack the riddle and BOOM! We will have
our items."

The riddle was twelve lines, and we had to find six
items. He gave me the riddle, and it read:

I appear wide, but lighter than air

The color of sun, hold me with gentle care

The next thing is hard, but slippery too

The color of anything, and something you use

But third you won't guess, it's small and it's nice

Anything you want, better check this twice

The fourth is tricky, maybe a ploy,

Dark and light, a radiant joy

Second to last, nothing to forget

It's a utensil to eat with, and something you set

The last is not a thing, not a doll but thin

Not an animal, not an item, showing some skin

"Okay, you all can leave! The first group back wins!"
Ms. B announced. The chairs in the cafeteria scraped the
floors and everybody was gone.

The riddle was very easy, in my opinion. I had fairly
good idea about what everything was, so then I looked at
Samuel and asked, "Okay- the first item- would you agree
that it's a yellow balloon?" He nodded his head.

"Where are we going to get the balloon?" he asked
me. I suddenly had a flashback from the day we had
managed to get ourselves into Ms. Doe's room. And then
it hit me. I took the list, and ran to the stairs to the top
floor. From the past, I knew we weren't allowed up on the
top floor, but I hadn't been exactly following them, had I?

"Just stand outside the door while I get it," I ordered
Samuel. While Samuel stood in front of the door, I sprang
into Ms. Doe's office, and it looked like she hadn't
touched a thing. The yellow balloon was still at the edge of

her desk where I had put it, and then I grabbed it, stuffing it into my pocket. A few seconds later, I appeared in the doorway, and I handed the riddle to Samuel.

"Okay, so 'the next thing is hard, but slippery too, the color of anything, and something you use'- have any idea what that is?" he asked me.

"Yes," I answered. "Soap." He thought about it for a second, nodding his head in agreement.

"Yes," he said. "That makes sense." Then we took off running down to the fourth floor where we went to the bathroom. We grabbed the soap, and I stuck it inside the balloon. We had two items, and needed four more.

"I don't get it- wide and light?" someone said passing us. A group of about six came hurdling into the bathroom, but I was sure they didn't know what they were looking for.

I pushed Samuel out of the way, and then leaned into him, whispering, "I think the fifth item is like a spoon or something, but I don't get the radiant joy thing."

He glanced at the riddle again, and grabbed my hand, pulling me with him. At first I didn't know where we were going, but then we were in his room. He hopped onto his bed and pulled down his ceiling. Reaching his hand into the ceiling, he pulled out a flashlight and chucked it at me. "Check this," he said. "Does it match up?"

He pulled our riddle down, and sure enough, it appeared that it could be the item they were looking for.

"Well," I said. "Lets go down and get the utensil, and then we'll be almost done." Samuel agreed and then after a few flights of stairs, and a few breaths I had to catch up on, we were down in the dining hall.

"Where are we going to get it?" I asked him, frantically looking around. I felt like we were behind because the room was vacant.

"IN THE CORNER!" he shouted, taking off to the corner of the room. We didn't know which utensil they were looking for, so we grabbed all three: a knife, a spoon, and a fork.

In the corner, I set out the four items we had collected, scratching off them in the riddle. "I don't get the third item, or last," I said to Samuel, who was checking the riddle with me.

"'It's small, its nice, anything you want, better check this twice," he muttered to himself, reading off the riddle.

he studied it for a little bit longer, and then shouted, "I've got the last two!"

"What are they?"

"Let's go get your teacher, then I'll tell you!" he laughed, disregarding my question.

"Tell me what?" a voice intervened, but it was Ms. B, which was good because it saved us some time from finding her.

"We're done!" he screamed, waving his hands in the air.

"Well let me grab Allison and we'll start looking your items over," she informed us. Then Ms. B disappeared and left the dining hall, returning several minutes later with Ms. Doe.

"These two were the first to finish," I could hear Ms. B explaining to Ms. Doe. "They surprised me, honestly-they came back so fast!"

As they drew closer to us, Ms. Doe appeared to be looking very pleased with herself.

Why?

"Why- I am so shocked that you two were the first to finish!" she said sarcastically. She ran her fingers through her hair, and put them firmly on her hips. "Let me see it then, the items that you have found so quickly!"

I indicated to the eating utensils we had, the yellow balloon, the soap, and the flashlight, but I turned to Samuel to take the rest of it away.

"The other item is her earrings," he proclaimed, pointing to the studs in my ears, and then said, "The other is you, Ms. Doe, or Ms. B."

Ms. Doe looked over our items, looking clearly impressed, while I stood to the side wondering how Samuel had figured the rest out.

"Very nice," she uttered. "Very nice. But do tell me how you found these items?"

I bitterly wish I could have said, "Where's our prize?" but didn't because I knew I would have ticked her off her rocker. Instead, I started describing the places where we found them, minus the balloon, which I left out.

"And the yellow balloon?"

"I had S- I mean E5- follow me up to the top where

he informed me we couldn't be up there. The yellow
balloon was right at the top of the stairs- but at that point-
I didn't know we needed a balloon. But," I lied. "I picked
it up anyway."

I looked at her with my face wallowing up into anger.
I didn't expect her to ask where we had found the items,
but rather just let her see them.

"Really, now?" Ms. Doe asked. She leaned down to
about a head away from us, looking intently into our eyes.
"I recall only having one balloon in the building. Do you
expect me to believe-"

"Oh-come on, Allison. A deal is a deal," Ms. B
barged in, standing up a little straighter. If I were the six
feet height of Ms. Doe, I probably wouldn't have taken her
seriously.

Ms. Doe relaxed, and huffed loudly, exposing her
deadly teeth. "Okay- well, lets round up everybody, then,"
she furiously raged. She stalked off, leaving Ms. B in the
room with us.

"I have to admit," Ms. B started speaking. "That was
some record timing- I think." She nodded her head at us,
and started walking away.

"I'm going to go and help Allison," she called, as she opened the dining hall door. When it completely closed, I turned to Samuel.

"Ms. Doe knows about us going into her office," I said to him. "I think she purposefully made the riddle up, just to include one yellow balloon. I bet there is no other place in Incognito to find a yellow balloon."

Samuel sat down in the chair closest to him, leaning back and shutting his eyes. After a few minutes, he opened them, and said, "I think you're right." Right when he admitted that, Ms. Doe came barging into the room again with a sizeable group of people.

"Sorry to say this, but E5 and Samantha have won," she sourly spit out. All the kids' faces started sinking.

"What!"

"I only got three of the items!"

"Man, we were so close! Just that stupid balloon left!"

They all sat down while Ms. B and Ms. Doe stood up at the front, waiting for everybody to be quiet.

"Hush everybody," Ms. B screamed. She cupped her hands around her mouth to make it louder and more forceful, and it did work the room fell silent

"Well, lets have a round of applause for them," Ms. B cheered. She started clapping, and the rest of the girls and boys clapped too. Ms. Doe clapped as well, but just enough to say that she did clap, other than that, her index fingers barely moved back and fourth.

"The winners," Ms. B continued. "Gets to have a tour of some of the places in Incognito that aren't allowed to be seen by any of you, like Ms. Doe's office, and certain other rooms.

"Samantha, E5, why don't you head along with Ms. Doe where she can start your tour," Ms. B finished. I looked over to Samuel and made a funny face at him.

Great, I thought. *This is the prize we get.*

Ms. Doe stood up and started leading us out of the dining hall. She didn't say anything as we left, and when I thought she was leading us towards the stairs, she was taking us to an elevator.

"I never knew you had elevators here," Samuel said, shocked. Ms. Doe pressed the button, and then when it opened and we were safely inside, she looked at us and said, "I'm sure you would have known."

"What's that supposed to mean?" I bitterly asked Ms. Doe.

"Like you don't already know," she spat back. The elevator dinged and then we were up on the top floor, walking to Ms. Doe's office.

"You might as well make yourselves at home while were up here," she raged, opening the door to her office. "Or," she added. "It may be better just to take you somewhere different form here, and show you a new place here, if you haven't already seen it."

When we came in and sat in the office, Ms. Doe sat at the other side of her desk, and then looked upon us saying, "I hope you don't expect me to show you the rooms here, because I am not. You are two of the biggest brats I have ever met. Have I made myself clear?"

Her voice was filled with so much anger that it sound like she was going to murder us there right then on the spot. We looked at each other and then nodded our heads up and down.

"Good then. Well, you are free to go. And don't mention to anyone that you didn't see anything, because were here in my office, are we not?" she laughed cruelly, and then started to look at the papers on her desk.

I didn't know what to do from there, so I stood up and left the room with Samuel behind me. When we were far enough away, I looked at him and whispered, "She doesn't like either of us!"

"No she doesn't," he agreed with me. We were almost down to the bottom of the staircases, and then he recommended that we go and sit outside for a while. I agreed with him, and we ended up lying out in the grass until the sun went down, and it was time for dinner. It

CHAPTER 7.

The rest of the week played out nicely, and soared by. I avoided Ms. Doe at all costs, and I was extra careful about what I said to Samuel when we weren't alone, calling him names so that the government wouldn't suspect a thing.

I told Samuel everything, and he shared many secrets with me. I spent every moment with him for as long as I could, and most of the time, we spent our days outside walking around.

I didn't want to leave.

The morning of the ninth day came, and it was raining outside, so Samuel and me had to stay indoors.

I had arrived at the dining hall without even thinking, and was one of the first ones this time. But when I entered the room with the delicious smelling food, I saw Samuel, and there was a guard standing next to him.

It was Mal, the guard that opens the gate. She had long, stringy black hair, and black eyes. She stood about an arms-length from Samuel, looking at me; I think she suspected something.

"Hello, Sa- E5," I corrected. Mal stood awkwardly to the side, looking angrily at me. She didn't look like she was listening, just staring into space, yet I was very wary of what I said. Ms. Doe was right next to her.

"Oh, sorry it took awhile to get the guard, but I now have one with you two," Ms. Doe apologized.

"My trip is coming to a close, so we must finish fast." I had my notebook in my hands and pencil, but I hadn't written anything in them yet. The words in which Samuel and me spoke were too dangerous.

"I am ready when you are, Miss," he said back to me. He sounded very monotone, and looked at me under his hair that covered his eyes.

Samuel turned from where he was standing, and started directing us towards the exit. I followed him, and Mal followed me at a very close distance. And that's how it was the whole entire day.

Wherever Samuel went, I went, and Mal went. She sat with us outside when it stopped raining, and when we were inside, and when we were at lunch. She had a notebook of her own that she carried around with her throughout the day scratching nonsense down, and she didn't approve of something, so as it seemed, she would ask questions.

"What did you mean, the government didn't like that? You said what, you liked the olden century better?"

All in all, the only topic I discussed with Samuel was about how right the government was while he agreed, and he even called himself an abomination. Therefore, we did not have a productive day.

The next morning was even worse. Mal had another guard with her, a guard that was just as ugly, as cruel, and as stupid as she was. But I wasn't going to put up with it, and I didn't.

Samuel and I were walking down the hallway, Mal and the other guard flanking the sides of us. They had been questioning us the whole time while I tried questioning Samuel, so I stopped. Samuel did too.

"Why'd you stop? Keep movin'," Mal snapped, looking back at me.

"I don't want you following me around!" I declared. Mal looked disgusted; she must've never been called out before in her life.

"DON'T YOU EVER-"

"What's going on here?" Ms. B interrupted. She had popped out of nowhere, standing in the doorway of one of the nearest doors on this hallway to us. I was hardly ever thrilled to see Ms. B, but here she was.

She looked exhausted; her curly blonde hair was in a messy bun hanging at the nape of her neck; her eyes were really red and bloodshot, like she hadn't had any sleep; her skin clung to her body, but was very dirty. I spoke very softly to her.

"Ms. B, I cannot possibly work on the research part of my essay when these two guards are constantly with us."

"Well, I suppose you're right," she agreed, turning towards the two guards. Her voice toughened up a little bit when she said, "I am guessing that you're going to leave her alone now, right? This is for a major assessment, and if she wins, she will give her speech during the Women's Revolution Day Parade. I can't have you two messing up her chances of winning."

"Sorry, mam, but it is under Ms. Doe's best wishes and desires that we watch E5. We are not supposed-"

"No, you will. You will turn your backs and walk the other way. We will be gone by tomorrow afternoon, and then you can go back to watching him. Are we clear?" She asked.

"We cannot turn our backs, mam, but we will stay at a respectful space behind, okay," Mal stated, but she looked like she wanted to rip Ms. B apart.

Ms. B smiled and disappeared through the door in which she had come out of, leaving Samuel and me with the guards. I turned my head to watch Mal take twenty steps back, every step pounding the floor even further than before. The other guard, unwillingly, stepped back, but not as far.

"I'm going to report this, you know!" I heard her utter behind us.

"I'm sure you will," Samuel said under his breath, chocking down a laugh.

We continued down the hallway until we reached one of the doors to go outside. It was our best chance of talking without the guards hearing us.

"OKAY E5," I shouted, so the guards could hear me. "What, exactly, do you like about this wonderful facility?"

I cocked my head to the side to make sure I could see the guard's reaction to what Samuel said.

"I don't know, Samantha, that's a tough one. It could be the food, or the punishment... Well, I think it's both. Life is dandy, and it is the way things should be," Samuel responded, sort of in a mockery tone, but very subdued and serious that the guards seemed to approve.

"You're really good at this," I whispered to him.

"Well, since I have always been here, you eventually learn," he said back. "And thanks for the compliment," he added, nudging me with his elbow.

"DON'T YOU DARE TOUCH ME!" I playfully screamed at him. A split second of fear washed across his face, but then vanished as he saw my expression.

"Do you we need to be of assistance to you, Samantha?" one of the guards shouted. I looked back at them and put my thumb up in the air, shaking my head no.

"Well, I have a really good feeling that I will be coming back. I don't know when, but I am going to make it," I promised. The sun was out, shining heavily making on my pale skin it hard for me to see. Samuel shifted so his back was to the sun, and looked at me.

"Hey, do you think you could you distract the guards for me, for a few minutes?" Samuel asked suddenly. He seemed excited for something.

"I don't know how I will-"

"Just trust me."

I took one of my earrings out of my ears and put it into my pocket while Samuel tore a piece of paper from my notebook and ran into the building.

"I HAVE TO USE THE BATHROOM," he shouted from a distance, entering Incognito. I waved to the guards who came running towards me with their guns.

"Anything wrong?" one of them asked, with their armed forces ready. They were looking frantically around me.

"No, no! I- uh- I have lost my mom's earing that she gave to me- uh- it's really important to me!" I lied. I held my breath, and hoped they wouldn't look down into my pocket where a big bulging item was.

The two guards were on their hands and knees helping me search for a few minutes sifting through the grass. When I had my chance, I slipped the earing out and tossed it in their direction.

"Oh, Miss, is this your earing?" one of them cheered, holding up a sparkling diamond so that I could see it.

I beamed at them and flashed my white teeth, emphasizing my gratitude and thanking them, proudly shoving the earing back into my ear.

"What'd I miss?" Samuel bellowed across the land. He jogged up to me while the guards muttered something in disbelief about how he was the one who took my earing. I just stared at him shaking my head, rolling my eyes.

"Okay, so I left you something under your bed," he whispered. How he got to my room was a mystery, but that left me puzzled. What did he do?

"Just make sure you don't let anyone see what you have," he warned me. "If you're caught, I'm dead, and you… I don't know." He shook his head, and motioned for me to follow him. We ended up back inside and pretending like we were working.

I used my notebook to sketch a few drawings; what I found was neither unconvincing nor invigorating. Samuel could not draw, and how he sees women is funny. He drew a woman with horns on her head, and on the butt he drew a tail that looked like an arrow. When I asked him what he was trying to symbolize, he said it was the devil. Apparently that was something to do with who his religion, so I let it go.

■■■

After I ate dinner, I walked up to my room with Lyanna behind me. O2 had told her she was pretty, and she got upset, so she stammered off to bed without saying anything. She was so dead asleep by the time I had gotten ready to crawl into bed that she didn't know I had the light on, and that I was trying to search for what Samuel had hidden.

He had said – or maybe he didn't mention it at all- that what he was giving me was under something, so I checked the bed.

I screamed.

I was holding a book! But not just any book, a book from a long, long time ago. It was a really flimsy book; the words and artwork on the front page were faded. But after tilting it several different ways in the light, I made out the title of the book and it read "Dear John."

John? Is that a boy's name? I asked myself.

I opened the book and started reading it immediately. Not only did the back of the book say that it was a romantic novel, but it was written by a boy!

I couldn't keep my eyes off the pages. They meant so much, yet were nothing but a hundred of pages of words that could easily disappear into nothing.

I didn't want to give the book back, or for it to disappear, so I stayed up all night long, reading each line carefully over and over again, so I wouldn't miss a thing.

How could a woman and man be in love with each other? I asked myself. That isn't normal!

But before long, the night was over, and the morning crept up on me so quick that I didn't get any sleep. I had had breakfast, and fallen asleep twice on the breakfast plate. However Ms. B giving her speech had waked me back up twice, and eventually I cave din and listened to it.

"It has been such an honor to be here the passed week," she said. "It's too bad we have to leave early, but it has been a memorable trip. I hope to see you all soon." She stepped down from the podium, and soon we were all walking outside. Out luggage was already being place onto the little golf cart a head of us.

When we got to the edges of Incognito, the little golf-cart bus roared to life in it's little engine, and picked us all up. Samuel, and a few others, stood at edge of the steps of the front doors of Incognito watching us all leave. Samuel, on the other hand, was bouncing his hand on his head, which was our new way of waving.

I watched him and the rest of the boys down at the edges become smaller and smaller as the bus trundled up the hill until they were a little tiny line in the distance. Then the golf cart passed through the gates, where Carson and Ellison were, and on the train we all went.

CHAPTER 8

The train ride home was dull. Lyanna didn't talk at all; she just sat next to me, sleeping in her long, polka dot pajama pants, snoring away. I gazed out the window the whole time, watching the farmland mutate into crowded forests of thick trees, and then into the buildings of the subdivisions that seemed to spring to life.

The train slowed, and then I found myself walking out of the blue train, walking down the steps, walking to my mom, who stood outside waiting with other anxious mothers, smiles plastered over their faces.

All the senior girls were screaming at each other and laughing and talking about the trip; they didn't understand like I did; they couldn't see past the government's wall like I could.

I spotted my mom in the distance; she looked bigger than she normally did. Not the kind of bigger where she gained extra weight, it was all in her stomach. But I wasn't going to mention that, not just yet.

When I grabbed my large suitcase and fought my way through the crowd, the only thing my mom said to me was, "We'll talk when we get back home," when I came to her and hugged her.

She knew, I thought. *She knew that I knew something.*

And before I knew it, we were back home. She had made soup earlier that day, and had two bowls of it steaming on the kitchen table. She sat at one end, and I sat on the other.

"I call him Samuel now," I said to my mom, but I kept my voice real low.   Her brown eyes twinkled with curiosity.

"Call whom, what?"

"You said you wanted to name your first child Sam, so I named him."

She dropped her spoon in the bowl, broth spilling over the sides while tears weld up inside her eyes. I had gotten her attention.

I told her all about Samuel and Incognito, while she listened intuitively. I told her about Ms. B and her possible sons that she visits, and everything that happened. The last thing I said caught her off guard, and possibly me too.

" I'm getting Samuel out, mom," I said strongly. I noticed how I didn't say how I wanted to get him out, but how I was going to get him. I felt so proud of myself.

"Sam, I will not allow that, even if I want to see Samuel myself."

"No, I am, mom, and there's nothing you can do to stop me. You know as well as I do that you want to see him free, and besides, you have already seen him before," I yelled. Anger was rising in me, and rising fast.

"What? I haven't seen-"

"Don't deny it mom. He was able to give a full-out description about you. He said you were the nicest women he had ever seen, and it made him rethink his prejudices against women. You changed him! You have to help me, were going to get him out and the rest of them!"

My soup bowl sat deserted on the table. The only sound in the room was my heavy breathing and my mom's gasps she let out every two seconds.

"I don't- I mean I went their once but it was for my job. It meant nothing. I mean, I remember seeing and thinking that he resembled you, I ditched the thought as soon as it struck. I wasn't going to let that get in the way of you," she said in muffled sobs. She hung her had in shame, and looked up, and said nothing.

"Fine, if you don't want to help me, I'll do it myself-"

"Fine," she breathed out, "I'll help you."

~

The rest of the night was quiet. My mom sat in the living room reading, and I worked on the essay; and I wrote it all wrong.

I was supposed to write about how the government was right, and has been right ever since the women took over, but I said it was in the wrong. I was supposed to write about the boys as creatures, but I wrote about them as being equals.

This was the first step in rebelling all I've ever known, but I had a pretty good feeling that Ms. B would like my essay and send me back. She needed to send me back; I had to go; it was important to me, to my mom, to her.

~

School the next morning was uneventful. History was stupid because we talked about Ms. Doe the whole time and how great she is; I felt awkward during the whole conversation because most everybody agreed with Ms. Warren. Trigonometry was easy because it was all review, and science was cancelled because my teacher had called in sick, so, because I had nothing better to do, I went to Ms. B's room.

When I found my way to her room, which was on the top floor of my school, she was back in the classroom at her desk. Her head was bent over exposing her white scalp, and scribbling noises accompanied her hand movement.

"Hello Sam," she greeted me, looking up from the papers. "You do know that class doesn't start for another hour, right?"

Her big brown eyes followed me as I sat down, waiting for me to respond.

"That's why I came to see you."

She put her pen down on her desk, and folded her hands neatly on top.

"I'm listening," she said.

I leaned into her desk, resting my elbows on either side of me, and whispered," I am going to get the boys out, and I need as many people as possible who can help me."

Ms. B's brown eyes widened with fear; she looked as if she had just chocked on something.

"Sam! Don't you ever say something like that! You should be glad that I don't report you-"

"I know why you won't report me, Ms. B," I sneered. "What are their names again? Jeremy and Michael, is that right?"

"How dare you accuse of me of having a relationship with two boys!" she screamed. Her face was getting hotter, and redder, and if smoke could really come out of people's ears, she would have large mounds of it escaping her right now.

"Is everything alright?" a voice called from behind.

Ms. B and I both whipped our heads in her direction. It was Ms. Doe. How convenient.

"Yes, of course. Ms. Doe, how are you? Do please

come in for a second," Ms. B asked. She stood up from her desk and started walking over to Ms. Doe. I followed.

"I couldn't possibly, Ellison. I am actually on my way down to the town square. I must go sort out an issue with a little lady who has just given birth to a creature, and is quite upset; she doesn't want to give the thing up."

Ms. Doe smiled, and eyed the back desk where she saw the pile of papers Ms. B was grading.

"Ah, I see. Are we grading the essays from the facility?" Ms. Doe asked.

"I am, I am, and they are fabulous, too! I don't think we should have any trouble with this years group of girls," Ms. B answered.

There was hesitation to her voice, and I assume that Ms. Doe heard it as well, because she stepped into the classroom with her dinosaur legs, and walked back to the desk. She grabbed the stack of papers and started looking through them.

"Now where's Ms. Yards's?" Ms. Doe asked. She hit the end of the papers and looked at me.

As soon as I started answering, Ms. B butted in and

said, "Sorry, Ms. Doe, but I cannot let you see that one yet. I was just telling Sam that her paper is one of the best yet. I think she'll be going back to the facility."

My mouth dropped, but I closed it so Ms. Doe would suspect anything. Why was Ms. B saying that? Did she want to help me now?

"Well congratulations Ms. Yards! I cannot wait to read it!" Ms. Doe chimed. She put the papers down on the deck, her plastic smile on her face, and walked back to the door. She said her goodbyes to Ms. B and I, and then left, but before Ms. B said anything, she quietly shut the door.

"Do you know were going to do this?" Ms. B asked.

"So you're going to help me?"

"Yes," she answered.

Ms. B sat back down at her desk, and began grading the papers again. The bell rung, making me jump, but Ms. B didn't budge. She sat there unnerved and calmly like.

As all the girls staggered in, Ms. B whispered, "We'll finish this conversation after class," and then gradually made her up to the front of the classroom.

I found my seat, which was right next to Ms. B's

desk, and sat in it, staring off into space. The room filled quickly, only a few students trailing behind when the last bell rang. Lyanna was among the last few students who were later; she came and sat beside me.

"Did you finish your essay?" she asked me, pulling out her essay. It was only a page long, double-spaced. I smiled.

"Not to the extent of yours," I joked. I pulled mine out and set it down on the desk, but I flipped it over so she couldn't see it. I wasn't sure how she would respond to it.

"Good afternoon, class," Ms. B greeted us. She paused, waited for us all to say hello to her, and said, "I would like everybody to hand in their essay, please. Just pass them all to the front- thank you. I will be reading all the essays the rest of the week and weekend, and hopefully, if not by this Friday, by next Monday I can say which five people will be going back for a further observation."

I didn't pass my essay to the front, but rather sat it on Ms. B's desk, still face down. Lyanna noticed, but she didn't say anything for which I was grateful for that.

The remainder of the class was devoted to reading a book that Christy Labelle wrote, the woman who initiated the Women's Revolution. The book was very interesting itself, but I didn't make it far into it; my mind went from thinking about what Samuel was doing now to how I would to get him out. When the bell rang, I waited for everybody else to leave before speaking to Ms. B again.

"You do realize how dangerous this is, right?" Ms. B asked me. I laughed and began to wonder how many people were going to ask me this. "Yes, and yes, and yes. It isn't fair to them, and I think they deserve to be out with us," I said strongly. "Plus, my brother is in there. I want him home."

"How many people know about you wanting to break the men out?" Ms. B asked. She was scribbling words down onto a piece of paper, and then looked back up at me.

"Just you and my mom. And my mom's in on it too," I added.

Before Ms. B could say anymore, a knock on the door came, and a teacher opened it. She walked right on in, and a few others came too.

"Are you ready for the meeting, Ellison?" one of the teachers asked.

"Yes, I'll be ready in one moment. Just finishing up with my student," Ms. B responded.

She looked back at me and whispered, "Here, take this- and go home now."

She handed me a piece of paper, and pushed me along and out through the door, where I continued my journey until I was out of the school.

The outside was chilly and bright, too bright that I had to find a shady tree before I opened Ms. B's note. It said:

Meet me here on tomorrow afternoon: Subdivision 5, Ridgeway Road, 237, North of Scranton.

I put the note in my pocket, and walked home, which was very quick and easy today. The sidewalk was vacant, and there were hardly any cars on the road.

I didn't hear it at first, but there were cheering noises and what sounded like crowds of people. So, after I unlocked the door and put my things down, I left to find it, which wasn't hard to find.

The large crowd of people was at the very end of my street; the part where my street turns from a neighborhood into buildings and officers. There were thousands of women screaming and shouting, and some had signs, but I couldn't read them.

I made my way through the crowd, pushing through everybody, and found the center of it. Christy Pepper, the head of First Division was there with a microphone in her hand, chanting.

"Last night, one of our own, good people, tried to help one of the creatures escape! Why? I have know idea," Christy Pepper raged.

She was a short woman, but in her heels, she seemed intimidating. The plumpness of her body was highlighted by the plain black dress she wore, which hugged her figure so tightly I wasn't sure how she could walk, and talk, at the same time. She circled the helpless woman, spitting around her, and making angry noises.

"Here is the person who is responsible for this," she pointed at a woman sitting on the ground; her hands and feet were tied together with rope.

"Why would you ever think to do this?" Christy Pepper yelled.

The woman lay there, and was quiet for a minute. She looked up at Christy Pepper and just stared at her with a smirk on her face and spat, "Like you don't already know!"

"DON'T USE THAT TONE WITH ME!"

"THEN TEL YOUR PEOPLE WHAT REALLY HAPPENS!"

Christy Pepper slapped the woman's face hard, hard enough for me to hear, and enough of the crowd to hear to all gasp.

"This woman right here, everybody, has forgotten what it was like back one hundred years ago. She doesn't seem to get that we, the woman, were all suffering! The men treated us like dirt! The men forgot that we were the reason why they lived. Without women, men wouldn't exist! It's a tragedy that you don't see it," Christy Pepper sneered.

She called a guard to come out to her, and she took a gun out. She clicked the gun, and looked right at the woman.

"This, everybody," Christy Pepper said, "Is what happens when people like her, disobey me! When people like her disobey the laws that have kept this glorious land running without fault for the past hundred years. I hope this is a little lesson nobody else has to share."

Christy Pepper clicked the gun, and the woman fell, her lifeless body lying there.

I left right away, while some of the other woman screamed and cheered for Christ Pepper's action.

Tears streamed down my face while I ran home in the brisk autumn air. My body was protesting what I would be doing, but I had to fight it. I had to fight it for the women who have suffered killings by that woman did. It wasn't right.

Once I found my little rectangle of a home, I got in and locked the doors. My mom was there already, cooking dinner, but I ran straight to her and cried. I told her what Christy Pepper did, and hugged her until I could no longer cry anymore.

When I released my mom from the hug, I noticed her core looked wider. I looked at her, pointing at her stomach.

"I was going to tell you, but…" She left the sentence hanging.

"So you're having a baby?" I asked her.

"There's a problem, sweetie," my mom admitted. She put a pan in the oven, set the timer, and made her way to the couch. I followed her and sat beside her; her eyes were sad.

"It could be a boy."

She said it quick, and dropped her head. I gasped. *What did this mean?* I asked myself. *What could this mean? Would she give it up?*

"And if it is a boy, you're not going to give it up this time," I proclaimed. I wasn't going to let her this time.

"No," my mom gasped. She put her hands on to her stomach, and then looked back up to. "Not this time."

We sat in a few minutes of silence, letting the

soundless room was over us. Then without warning, my mom said, "Tomorrow we will find out. An appointment has been scheduled, so be ready in the morning, okay?"

I said okay back to her, and left to go to my bedroom. I didn't do much in my room, just sat and stared at the ceiling, imagining a world where boys and girls walked among each other. I smiled and fell into a deep sleep, questioning society.

~

The next morning I woke up with eyes that didn't look like eyes. I lackadaisically pulled on an oversized sweater and leggings due to the fall-like air that was coming in, and by the time I had choked down a banana, my mom was ready to go. Before we met up with Ms. B, we had to run some errands, so the next thing I knew, I was being dragged into store after store.

First we went to Subdivision Square where the riot had happened yesterday. It is one large square where shops border the inside; in the middle of it is a fountain of Christy Labelle, and all the people who have been Head of

First Division at her feet. Christy Pepper was one of them.

She was one of the most recent statues to be added to the fountain, and was the most ugly of all the statues. Her nose had been enlarged, and so had her hands so that now they look like guys hands. I laughed quietly to myself.

My mom needed to do some grocery shopping, so while she went off into Peppers and Onions, I wandered around, window-shopping. After circling the property twice, I concluded that there wasn't much to see, or buy for that matter. If I wanted to, then I guess I could have used five minutes of time staring at tools that I have no use for, so I just passed it and kept walking.

Ten minutes passed…no mom…. Five more minutes… no mom. I was beginning to think she wasn't in there, so I went in myself, walking the isles. I filtered through isle after isle, and still had no luck, but then a woman's voice startled me.

"There you are!"

The voice didn't sound like my moms, but I still looked, but nobody was there. Then I turned to the west side of shelves, and peered through the different boxes of food where I saw a few women I didn't know, and one that I heard much about; none other than Christy Pepper.

She hugged a sour-looking woman and draped her arm around her, continuing walking down the isle. Maybe I shouldn't have done what I did, but I followed.

I only heard bits and pieces of her conversation at first, but it was only the trivial "Hello, how are you...Yes, I am doing well too," that I missed. They made there way outside while I stayed behind them, forgetting about my mom.

" So, are you going to do what I asked to?" Christy Pepper asked. She sat down on the fountain side, the other woman sitting next to her. I sat on the opposite end, where the big statue blocked their view from me.

"Yes, I have. The order is in, and the approval will no doubt be here soon," the other woman promised. I couldn't see their faces, but the discomfort of the woman was evident.

"Are you ready?"

I looked up and saw my mom walking out of Peppers and Onions with two bags of groceries. As she drew nearer to me, the shuffling of feet approached me, and Christy Pepper stood right in front of me.

"Oh, Sam- it is Sam, right?- it's so good to see you!" Christy Pepper greeted. She gave me a big hug and turned towards my mom who joined me.

"How are you doing?" she asked my mom, resting her hand lightly on her shoulder.

"Very good, thank you. It's so unlikely to see you Ms. Pepper, without any guards. Where are they?" my mom smiled.

"Oh- you know- they're just walking around. I really just wanted to come and see my statue," she responded. She made a hand gesture that suggested she was pointing to her statue, where she looked back at us.

"Well," Christy Pepper began. "I must be going. I have to get back to work." She shifted back and forth on her feet, and smiled again. "Have a good rest of day!"

As my mom turned to walk back to the car, Christy Pepper put her hand out in front of me and bent down to my ears and said, "I hope I don't see more of you in the future. It would be an awful shame."

I walked away from her, and when I turned to look back at her, she had her eyes on me, staring me down. My mom stood at the gate, leaning against her shoulder with her groceries in her hands.

"What did she want to say?"

"She just wanted to wish me good luck on my essay," I answered, lying in between my teeth. I smiled weakly and soon enough, we were in the car and driving. I grabbed the little piece of paper Ms. B had given me yesterday, and we started heading to where we were going to meet her.

"Okay, we're here," my mom said to me. I held up the little piece of paper with the address, and matched it too that of the house we were parked in front of. Sure enough we were at Subdivision 5, Ridgeway Road, 237, North of Scranton.

Did Ms. B want us at her house?

She had an extremely long driveway bordered by the grass that dies in the winter months; it was brown, and lined her whole house. By the looks of her house, it appeared to seem as nobody live here; the windows were boarded up with curtains in front of them, there were signs saying to go away.

"I don't think anybody lives here, mom," I said to her. I walked around the house, but there were no signs of life, just signs of green paint chipping off the sides.

"Well don't give up that easily!" my mom replied, knocking on the door. She didn't answer- let alone anybody answer- so we started heading back to the car.

Creek!

"Sorry, I am here!" a voice screamed from behind the garage door. The white door was slowly rising, revealing a big, white van behind it, with chains strapped to the tires, and Ms. B right beside it.

"Please come in," she said, waving her arms at us. I followed Ms. B through her garage, which was filthy. Besides the white van, boxes of cluttered, old items filled every space that she could fill.

"Sorry for the mess," she apologized, wiping her shoes off the welcome mat. "I don't usually have visitors."

She unlocked the door, and we entered her home. When she flicked on the lights, I was stunned by what I saw! All over the kitchen she had posters that said 'down with the government' and 'Cut Up The Peppers!'. If her way of expressing herself got in the wrong hands, she would be executed.

"You have a very lovely home," my mom said, complimenting Ms. B, but when she looked at me, she

hung her head and rolled her eyes.   *What had we*
gotten ourselves into?

"You have two sons, Jeremy, and Michael," I
randomly busted out. I didn't know what I had said until
the words slipped my tongue, so I curled my fingers over
my lips.

"And I believe you have a brother name E5 whom
you call Samuel, is that correct, Miss Yards?" Ms. B replied
back. She motioned for us to sit at the kitchen table while
she boiled some water.

"Yes. Then we're on the same page then?" I asked.

"Indeed we are," she answered. The sound of
something clicking clicked and Ms. B filled three mugs
with hot, steamy water. She put some tea bags in them,
and brought them to the table.

"How do you think we should go about this?" my
mom piped in. Her brown eyes narrowed straight into Ms.
B; if I didn't know any better, I would have assumed that
she didn't trust her yet.

"Well, the only people game on this is you," she
explained, pointing to me, "And you," she said, pointing to
my mom.

"So you don't have anybody else who feel the way we feel?" my mom asked.

"Not that I am aware of, so no," Ms. B replied. She took a sip of her tea, and then said, " But what we need to do is

CHAPTER 9.

All signs of autumn had vanished by the time December arrived. The chilly air rolled in, and winter break ended up starting earlier than expected. Three feet of snow bombarded us from the north just two weeks before Christmas, so naturally, with people not working, and schools getting closed, the spirit of the holiday season heightened.

The day that it had snowed during school, we had been released early. And it just so happened that Lyanna followed me home that day, not something she would particularly do.

I decided that partly because she was bored out of her mind I would do something unfathomable, something that I didn't think I was ever going to do, or would do.

I gave her 'Dear John'.

I didn't have a problem giving it to her, because she was one of those types of people who went with the flow. I knew it was a stretch when I gave her the book because sometimes she can be a bit aggressive on her beliefs, but I felt confident that she would fall in love with it.

"What's this?" she had asked, flipping the book around and around. The faded colors of the front and dusted pages of the book were bland as bland could get; she blew some of the dust off, exposing the cover, her face in shock.

"Well, before you get angry-"

"You mean I'm going to get angry?"

"Before you decide not to read it-"

"Oh I'm not going to READ it-"

"Before you tell somebody-"

"STOP! Don't do this to me now! I can already see it," she yelled and whispered and babbled. She waved her hands in the air, forming a box. "Local girl in Subdivision five caught with a mysterious book. Where did she get it? I don't know, it was a mystery…"

I waited for her to stop talking, as she shoved the book back into my arms. I withheld form giving it back to her, and tried to persuade her again.

"Sue me if you don't like it," I said, giving the book back to her. She yanked it out of my arms, and looked at me. "Do with it as you please, but I know you're curious.

Isn't everybody? This is a once in a life time chance..."

" I can consider it," she weighed in, "but where did you get it? How?" She demanded, folding her arms across her chest with the book.

I didn't expect for her to ask me that question, so I sat there holding my tongue, passing the time. "If I tell you, you won't believe me."

"Let's hear it then," she said in a mocking tone. Her leg was extended to the side, her hip out, and her body faced towards me.

"Samuel is-"

"Who is Samuel?" she fearfully asked.

"Samuel is the boy I had to watch, E5, as he was called by Ms. Doe. He is- how do I put this- well- brother- yeah, he is my brother," I answered, hoping that she would just blow all this off and laugh.

Okay, so she laughed, and she didn't believe me, like I had said.

"Yeah, that sound's like you, making up a lie," she chuckled. "But seriously, don't joke about this kind of stuff. This is what gets you into trouble."

She held the book admiring it cautiously, holding it a great distance away from her, like it was going to bite. I didn't know what to say.

"I'm being serious. Samuel is my brother, and he slipped this book underneath my bed the last night we were there. I read the whole thing that night, and it's honestly the best book I have ever read. It is so different from-"

"So what, exactly, did you do the whole time we were at Incognito? Didn't you take notes about what you were observing?" she interrupted, put her hands on her hips.

"You know it's okay to call him Samuel," I informed her. "And I was quite busy at Incognito. You would never believe what I saw."

"Of course I wouldn't," she stated.

"Well," I paused, letting her have a moment before I asked her the big question. "What I want you to do is help me out. I am officially going to try and get the boys out."

Lyanna whipped her head around, making her black hair fly everywhere. "WHAT?" she screamed. "ARE YOU EXPECTING ME TO HELP YOU?"

She stood up and looked at me like I had just said she was going to have to run the mile, flailing her arms in every direction.

"Actually, I figured that you would eventually succumb to what I am planning to do, so you might as well help me now then help me later. The rewards will be far greater than you think," I explained. Her face was turning darker shades of green; she still looked like she wanted to barf.

"I won't do it," she claimed, cocking her head to the side.

" You can have dinner with me tonight."

"What exactly are you having?" she inquired, lifting her brown eyelids at me.

"Does it matter?" I countered back while I cracked a smile.

"Okay I'll do it."

She took the book with her and went over to the couch, where she opened the front page. I stared at her in disbelief.

"What?" she asked me, as I came over, staring at her.

"Nothing, it's just that I thought you didn't want to read the book."

"Oh, well, I figured that since I am now a rebel, I might as well live up to who I am supposed to be."

~

Surprisingly, Lyanna finished the whole book, coming over the following day to rant to me about how much she loved it. It was strange having her do this, considering just the other month she had resented O2, but now, I think her eyes had been opened up to a far, greater world, which had existed.

She was officially on board now, whether she approved of it or not, and was actually starting to realize that the government had been wrong the whole time. I let a deep smile sink onto my skin.

When Christmas Eve arrived, I had not shopped for my mom yet, and we still had not gotten our tree. So, at the last minute, I did all my shopping Christmas Eve, and we got a tree. By the time we finished decorating the tree it in the white and red lights, and for my sakes, wrapping the presents, the clock had struck way passed midnight.

Because it was Christmas morning, I woke up at six, just barely scratching the surface of five hours of sleep. But it was always fun on Christmas morning, waking up and opening your presents.

"Merry Christmas," my mom beamed. She came and gave me a big hug, walking us into the kitchen where she started making breakfast. While she cooked the eggs, I toasted the bread and whipped the butter, and soon we were eating our breakfast. Unlike every other day, we sat at the fireplace with it on next to the tree.

"I think you are really going to like what I got you," she explained through mouthfuls of food. Her brown hair fell all over her face, and wasn't properly brushed, which wasn't like her.

"I think you'll like what I got you," I said back. I shoved the last remaining crumbs into my mouth, and positioned myself in fornt of the tree. Today it was filled with many little gifts, wrapped, and cared for.

"Then shall we open presents?" she asked me, setting her plate down. I nodded while she bent down to grab a small box, and passed it to me.

The brown paper and red string easily slid off the

present, revealing an old picture frame from before the revolution. The designs on the side were very swirly and curly, reminding me of a sun, and there was a big S on the side, listing different words that start with S.

I laughed, because my moms present I got for her was similar. When she opened her little box up, her eyes lit up right away. I had gotten her a necklace that said S&S on it for Samuel and me. She put it on immediately, and was almost crying.

"I absolutely love it!" she cried. She disappeared into the bathroom; coming back several minutes later with a very wide, grin on her face, we opened up several more gifts, and the stockings. When I thought we had reached the end, my mom said, "Oh- No there is one more- I'll be right back."

She disappeared once more, into her bedroom, and came back holding a long, well-wrapped, present. She tossed me my last gift saying, "This one- I am positive- will be your favorite."

I held the rectangular gift, trying to think about what it could be, but couldn't come up with a good explanation. The gift was thick, too thick to be any clothing, and when I shook it, the box sort of shook and rattled. The sound was unfamiliar, and I couldn't detect it.

"What do you think it is?" my mom asked me, nudging my elbow. I looked at it again, shook it again, and flipped it around again. I goggled at the present, and looked back up at my mom, shrugging. When she gave me the okay look, I started tearing the present open very slowly while savoring every minute of it, and when I ripped the rest of the paper off, I screamed.

At first I didn't know what it was. Underneath the paper was what looked like a half-inch computer looking device, and beside it were several CD's that had names written down on them. There were also many pictures that had guys in them.

"What is this stuff?" I asked my mom, pointing to the computer looking device. "Where did you get all this?"

The pictures were amazing! I had never seen any of it before in my life. There were boys with other boys at the beach, and boys with girls at the movies. There were also a few pictures of a girl in a big, fluffy white dress, standing next to man dressed very nicely.

"All of this stuff is from a time capsule our family did before the Revolution," she answered. I was still looking at everything, trying to figure what it was.

"What's a time capsule?"

"There was a small box that our family made many years ago, and buried it in the ground, putting items of all sorts in them, like photos and videos. Then you wait many, many years, and open it up later," she answered. She picked up a few of the photos, and then sent them coming my way.

"Those," my mom said, indicating the pictures she gave me, "Are some pictures of our great-great-great-great-grandparents. There should be a date on the back- Oh- yes there is. The pictures were taken in 2017 right when the Revolution started. They have been passed down in our family for over one hundred years through the capsule."

The photos were thin and old. The colors – which I am sure had once been very bright- were dull. The boys looked so happy in these pictures, and they had no idea what was coming.

"The CD's are actually videos of our family talking about the Revolution. And that," she said, looking at the computer, "Is a DVD player from a long time ago that can actually play the CD's you have."

"Thank goodness they put one of those DVD players in them, because who knows how we would have watched it!" she made note, looking at the computer-device.

I picked up the DVD player and headed for my room. "Do you mind if I go watch a few of them?" I asked my mom, going over to her and hugging her tightly. "Thanks for the gifts! This has been the best Christmas yet!" I whispered.

I disappeared into my room and plugged the DVD player in, which was actually more confusing than it appeared. There was a plug to plug into the wall outlet, but there were red and white wires that needed to go somewhere else. In the end, I attached it to the television, which helped.

I picked the first CD and read:

Grandpa Johnny & Grandma Liv-2019

I slipped the CD in, assuming that that was how I was supposed to do it, and a clip came up and started playing immediately. An older man with the wrinkliest face I had ever seen popped up

"Now wait a second Johnny, let me get over there before you start speaking!" a woman's voice demanded;

her voice was strong, and fragile.

"I can do what ever I want, Liv!"

"I am just saying-Johnny," Liv snapped, appearing into the clip. She had a cane with her, and her white hair covered just the tip of her eyes. It looked almost like how a boy's hair is cut.

They were silent for a minute, sitting on a couch, looking to the right. Then a voice startled me.

"How do you feel Grandpa, about what's happening right now?" a young girl asked. She wasn't shown on the camera, but if I had to guess, she was about thirteen.

"What about it- it's ridiculous. It isn't actually going to happen you know. In a few years, the women will get over themselves and all will be where it should be," he finished stating. He pulled his glasses off and wiped the lenses off.

"What do you think, grandma?" the girl asked.

The older woman put her hand on her husband and just shook her head. She was adorable.

The young girl kept asking questions, and the old people kept answering them. They were slow when they answered, and slow when they moved; every movement was delicate and they never stopped talking. At the end, the girl asked one more question.

"Grandpa, Grandma, what do you want to tell our family in the future?" she asked them kindly.

Johnny and Liv shifted so that their bodies were angled towards the camera and made their faces really serous. They took a few breaths, and then Johnny spoke softly.

"Who ever is watching this, it is probably the year 2135 or near it. I have know idea what life is going to be like, but if the women gain control completely like they are trying to do right now, do something about it. Christy Labelle is a madwoman, but people are joining her. This cannot happen, do you understand me?"

I felt like Johnny was with me in the room actually asking me the question. He turned towards his wife and asked her if she had anything to say, and then she chimed in.

"Johnny said it all," Liv stated. " I would highly suggest that if you haven't done anything about your situation if the women are in control, do something. I don't want to see my grandsons in those facilities that they're talking about."

Liv wiped a few tears that fell from her eyes, and stood up, arguing with Johnny. The clip stayed on for a few seconds, and went completely black.

I sat back and couldn't believe what I had just watched. Johnny and Liv were my family, which was hard to even consider, because up until Samuel, males didn't exist in my life.

I searched through the rest of the videos and watched a live speech given by Christy Labelle that one of my family members had been to, which was excruciating to watch. The worst part of it was that she had n extraordinary amount of people rooting for her.

CHAPTER 10.

We returned back to school as if (As if what?) nothing had ever happened. History was still in session, as so English and math, and all was well. Lyanna, on the other hand, had been so engrossed in the book 'Dear John' that she constantly talked about it. Teachers who were, as a matter of fact, in favor of the laws Christy Labelle had put in were causing me a lot of stress because they were getting so close to catching Lyanna with the book, or talking about the book (What would happen to her? What would happen to me?). She hadn't returned the book yet to me; her claim was that she wasn't finished with the book, and she needed more time.

I found out that she- without my condolences, of course- ended up giving the book to a few people so that they could read it. I was furious at first, but in the end, it actually worked.

"They loved the book, Sam!" she cried as we walked home one day from school. This was unlike her to walk home with me, but she did.

"I gave the book to Mary, Elizabeth…" and then she listed off all the people that she had loaned the book to. "They really want to do something about it!"

My heart leaped, and if I could have leaped a full split,

I would have right then and there. I stopped dead in my tracks, and looked at her.

"Oh- yeah- well I guess I should let you know that you are due for a meeting in about seventeen minutes," she announced. She looked at me apolitically, but then gave me a smile as wide as she could and threw her fists up into the air.

I didn't say anything; I couldn't say anything; my mouth was paralyzed.

"Well, you probably should get going, don't you think?" she asked me, seriously.

"Get going to WHAT?" I retorted back.

"Your meeting, of course," she said profoundly, like I didn't know what I was talking about.

"No, I'm sorry, what I think you mean is that WE," I said, emphasizing the we, "have to get to our meeting!"

Lyanna tossed her black hair over her shoulder, and turned around. I had no idea where we were going, but I followed.

~

Almost exactly seventeen minutes later, and a few turns through the neighborhood, we arrived at a big house; a house that I had never seen, and a house I had never crossed by. It was a large white house, with shutters as black as black could get, trimmed in red. An iron gate surrounded the premise of their home.

"Come on in! You're the first people to arrive!" a voice called to us. I found the red front door and found a girl who I did not know.

"My name is Carly," she greeted me, giving me a hug. When she pulled away, I noticed that she was a very pretty girl. Her hair was long and brown, and while her eyes were bright green.

"I'm glad you're here," she added, walking Lyanna and me up and into her home.

I couldn't decide what I liked better; the high ceilings or how all the furniture matched and shined.

"The other girls should be here any moment," she said to us, leading us into the front living room. She had set up extra chairs surround the biggest chair with an array of food on a small table.

"Thank you," I said to her as I sat down. She pointed to the big, blue seat that was the biggest, most lavish of all the chairs in the room. I literally sunk down in the chair when I sat.

I looked at Lyanna who started snacking on some of the crackers set out of the table and whispered; "I can't believe you've gotten me into this. I don't even know what I am supposed to say!"

She finished chewing the crackers, took a swig of some pink liquid, and screwed her face up into an expression of shock.

"I can't believe you did this too yourself, too," she replied, biting into more crackers. "But seriously," she ranted, "If I were you, I would have thought this out. So I guess that is why I am here. Oh! And Ms. B knows about this meeting, too. I have already talked to her," she added.

I chuckled, but then grew really nervous because the doorbell chimed and then a swarm of girls entered; some that I knew, and others I didn't. Mary, the bossy girl with the shoulder length brown hair, came striding in first.

Rebecca, the quiet girl, bounced in talking wildly; her blue eyes looked unnaturally bigger today, and her white teeth were shining pearly white. A few other girls followed, and they all made their ways to sitting around me.

Carly clapped a few times, and then whistled, to draw the girl's attention. She then pointed to me, and said, "Please give your attention to Sam."

I was lost for words. I didn't know what I was supposed to say to them, or what not to say to them, so I stood up and cleared my throat.

"Your plan is spot on, Sam!" Lyanna sarcastically belted out. The girls laughed hard which gave me a few seconds to think. I took a deep breath in, and then began.

"Well, were all here for the same reasons I assume? And we read the book?" I asked them. Everybody nodded in agreement.

"Okay, " I breathed, "great! I was hoping that we could settle on a few things as a whole, so first I want to talk about why we are here. You," I pointed to Rebecca. "Tell me why you are here."

Rebecca stood up, and loud and proudly she stated, "I have secretly always wanted to go against the government. My mom isn't too fond about them, and after visiting Incognito, I was in shock. I was glad when Lyanna gave me the book and said this was happening a few weeks ago."

I nodded my head while listening to Rebecca, and caught a quick glance at Lyanna. So she had had this meeting planned for the past few weeks. I shook my head in her direction and gave her the evil eye.

"Thanks Rebecca," I smiled. I turned to another girl and pointed at her. "Why are you here, and what's your name?"

The girl I had pointed to was long and lanky with stringy blonde hair. She stood up and was really quiet.

"My name is Sophie and I read 'Dear John' and thought it was an amazing book." She sat back down and crossed her feet. Then I asked the rest of the girls who all had similar stories. When they were all finished I spoke again.

"The reason why I am doing this is because I found out that I have a brother, and he lives at Incognito," I admitted. Gasps exploded from the girls and everyone started whispering.

"WELL," I shouted. "Let's not get all gossipy, I am sure all of you have family there too, you just don't know it. Anyway, we need to set some goals. Does anyone have any suggestions?" I looked around at the girls and then added, "We also should have somebody writing this information down."

Carly jumped up and disappeared into her house reappearing seconds later with a pen and notebook in hand. She sat there with attentive eyes while Mary stood up.

"First we need as many people as we can get, because I'm not sure that you noticed this, but nine girls is not going to be enough to change our system," she boasted. She flipped her brown hair over her shoulder, and sat back down.

"I understand that, Mary," I agreed with her. "But

CHAPTER 11.

January was cold, but February was worse. The snow
made it harder for me to meet with W.A.R., and when we
did meet, it was for limited amounts of time; we never
accomplished much, but we were progressing, which is all
that really mattered. We were also starting to prepare for
May when the Women's Revolution Day Parade would
happen, and when some of us would go back to Incognito.

The videos my mom had given me for Christmas
were still fun to watch. One of the people mentioned
Valentines Day – the day of love- and if that holiday still
existed, it would have been today. But Christy Pepper
really surprised us all with unexpected news that was
broadcasted to everybody in First Division. We would now
have to pledge our allegiance to her and what she believes
in, oh how that was going to be challenging.

I was at my house when this happened, surrounded
by the original seven girls from January's meeting, and
three more girls who had joined us. We were gathered
around the living room when the television sporadically
turned on. I sighed, because it only ever did this when
important information needed to be shared by the
government, specifically, Christy Pepper.

"Good afternoon ladies. I am sorry to bother some of you on such a busy day like today is, but I have a new announcement. Next week on the twenty- first, every girl will have to pledge your allegiance to our government. Children under the age of ten will not participate in this pledging, but will have to when they come of age.

"Anybody who does not partake in this ceremony will be inquired upon by officials; the worst of you will be executed. I am sorry to have to do this to you all, because I do indeed believe that everybody loves how our system operates, but word on the street is that there are more people starting to resist. Now we can't have that, can we?" she asked, finishing her small speech. It was no shock to us because she was wearing her shade of yellow with her contrasting skin ruining it.

"What are we going to do?"

"Does she know about W.A.R?"

"Is someone in here a traitor?"

Questions upon questions started getting thrown out. I had bought myself a whistle from the store a few weeks back, so I blew it, and the girls hushed.

"What do you think we should do?" I asked them.

They all looked at me with scared faces, eyes sinking back into their sockets. "We're not stopping W.A.R just because Christy Pepper says, "more people are resisting." We have no way of finding out if she means us, so my advice to you is to not worry about it. We will go and pledge out allegiance just like everybody else, and we will mean every word!"

The girls still all looked at me like I was crazy, and then Lyanna started clapping and hooting. Soon I had everybody clapping for me, and a standing ovation.

"We should counteract what we're doing here," one girl suggested.

I looked around the room to find her and asked her what she meant by that.

"Well," she began, standing up so everybody could see her. "I think we should be extra aware of what's happening in our surroundings. Maybe we should start advocating for our society to stay united, that way Christy Pepper won't look at us as her prime suspect."

Mary's head nodded, and so did Rebecca's. A few other girls' heads followed in a similar fashion, and then Carly was scratching down on the notebook.

"Okay, so we're now going to pretend like were for Christy Pepper, goody," I confirmed.

The girls started standing up and leaving, one by one. The only one who lingered was Lyanna, and the rest vanished into the snowy grounds, foots steps everywhere.

~

The following few days were the coldest they had been in a long time. The temperature didn't rise above twenty degrees Fahrenheit, and the sun had stayed hidden behind the clouds since the day Christy Pepper made her announcement.

W.A.R. had done a very good job promoting unity for Christy Pepper. They constantly had signs with them, and two of them had even designed shirts for it.

One of the times that I had seen them outside with their posters was the day we took our pledge. Four girls were spread across the front of the Belle building, shouting different things.

"WE ARE ONE!"

"FIRST DIVISION NEVER DIVIDES!"

Mary was one of the girls who were holding a decorative sign, and I walked over to her with Lyanna.

"I love the sign, Mary!" I said to her, winking my right eye while Lyanna took a seat on the steps in front of the building.

""Thank you, I have been working on it for a few weeks now!" she responded extra enthusiastically, raising the sign even higher as a few strangers walked by. "Christy Pepper herself has seen the sign, too," she added.

I gave her a thumbs up and grabbed a hold of Lyanna, and walked into the building. We were going to help sort the names of people pledging today for Christy Pepper.

When we stepped in, a long, golden rug had been placed on the floor. Ahead of us were signs pointing us to the auditorium where the pledging would happen, and to smaller rooms. We veered to the left where one of the signs said the sorting room and went in. Christy Pepper was in there sitting in the corner.

"Welcome!" she greeted us. She came over to us giving us a big hug and when she let go, I noticed she was wearing yellow; what a surprise.

"Okay, so, what I want you girls to do is sort the all these names by age. I want girls ten to nineteen in one group; twenty to twenty-nine; and so on. Its right over there," she informed us, directing us to the side of the room, indicating to a stack of names.

"And by the way," she added as we turned to go over to the tables. "I love the girls outside of the building. Nice way to promote our government!" Christy Pepper left the room to go do something else while we sat down on the side of the room.

The table was long and had hundreds upon hundred of names scratched onto a scroll. We started sorting them. Lyanna had the age of the people's list, so I would take a name, ask her the age of the person, and then put it in a pile.

"Jennifer Martin?" I asked Lyanna, after a while of sorting. She looked through the list and until she found the name.

"Twenty-one," she answered. So I put her in the twenty's pile, then looked at Lyanna.

"This is purgatory," she complained. "So many

names, so many people."

"All you have to do is tell me their ages," I noted to her. I picked the last name, asked her, and we were finally done. I pulled the piles and tied them together in yellow ribbon.

"Oh goody, are you done?" a voice cheered and asked. We both looked up and saw Christy Pepper standing in the doorway. She had transformed into a dark, silky gown, hugging just the amount of skin in her core, flowing behind her. "It's time."

We left the piles of names sitting on the table and followed Christy Pepper out of the room. The hall that had the golden rug on it had been renovated into a room to look like a castle, with velvet and maroon colors striking the floor and ceilings. It was filled with tons and tons of girls dressed in dresses for formal events. I looked down at my informal dress that wasn't as nearly as nice as the girls surrounding me, and shrugged. They were filing into the auditorium, so we followed them.

The line seemed to take forever to enter the room, but when we did, the biggest room I had ever seen came to life. The auditorium's ceiling was about three stories high with thousands of little yellow lights, and two stories of seats. I couldn't tell how many seats were in the room, but if I had had to guess, I would have said around ten thousand.

Lyanna and me found a few seats in the middle of the auditorium that wasn't as crowded as the seats in the front, and sat down into them. They were comfier than I thought they would be, and a deep velvet color matching the outside hallway, but I couldn't tell in the half-darkness of the room.

The double doors shut with a *thunk*, and the crowd of people in the audience went mute. We saw Christy Pepper walking out on to the stage ahead of us, accompanied by two guards at her side.

"Welcome everybody!" She greeted the crowd, tapping the microphone a few times.

"I am so glad we could all make it here today on this fine morning of the twenty-first. I just want you all to know that I chose to be here at this ceremony than the others happening all over First Division. I felt like Subdivision five is a real important one, and close to my heart, since this is where I officially live.

"Why don't we get started then?" she asked the

crowd. Everybody roared and then the first pile of names was picked out one of the guard's pockets next to her and handed over to her.

"I am going to read off this list girls and have all them go out of the auditorium and follow the guards," she told us. I dozed off while she read our names, and then rose when Lyanna tugged on my shoulder. We got out of our comfy seats and followed what looked like a thousand girls.

The auditorium was pitch black, so there were guards separated about every twenty feet, until we reached the bright light barrier of the auditorium doors. There were swarms of guards out here, sending the girls out in blocks of a hundred.

This was going to be a long day.

I checked the clock and it only said noon, and then sat and waited with Lyanna in line. I checked the clock again, and it had only been half an hour. I started getting antsy, and eventually, after fifteen more minutes we were sent out on stage.

We followed one of Christy Pepper's top guards down a black hallway, lit by small lights on the ceiling. The chatter of Christy Pepper talking to the crowd was growing louder as we neared the end of the hallway.

"Okay everybody, I think this is our last group of ages ten to nineteen. Why don't we all stand up and give them a round of applause," Christy Pepper ordered as we all lined up on stage. She took the microphone off the stand and then started walking down our line.

"After I say the following, you will repeat, 'I pledge to Christy Pepper, under the government that we have, that I will follow you, and only you, from here on and out'.

"The way that our government works is by keeping our Division in order. The facilities are meant to protect us, and the inhabitants in the facilities. It is how we have been ruling for the past century and a half, and how we will continue. It is how my family has been running this society since the beginning of the Women's Revolution.

"I was named after my great-great-great-great grandmother Christy Labelle," she laughed cold-heartedly. She smiled a big, fake smile, and looked back at us. "And you all- like myself- probably have great family members who fought hard in the Women's Revolution. And that's what we need to keep in place; it is our duty to protect what our grandmothers and aunts from the past wanted.

"Thank you," she finished up, looking into the crowd, bowing. She then looked at the first girl at the end of the line and said, "Now you may begin repeating your pledge. The words are over there if you forget." She pointed across the whole entire auditorium where, at the end of the room, there was the pledge being projected on the wall.

The first girl read her pledge, and then exited with a small bow. It continued like this all down the line until it got to me. The spotlight turned my way, and Lyanna passed the microphone to me. I read aloud.

"I pledge to Christy Pepper, under the government that we have, that I will follow you, and only you, from here on and out'."

I exited the stage by one of the guards and tried to keep my face poised. I did not want to show my anger or resentment to that pledge, because who knows what will happen when W.A.R. starts something.

Before another list was read off, they let us all find our seats again in the auditorium. I had to push several people out of the way as Lyanna and me found our seats again, and when everybody had found them, Christy Pepper read another long list of names off. This group was girls from twenty to twenty-nine, and then a flock of women exited the room.

"I am so glad we get to do this today," Christy Pepper said to us. She walked around, staring viciously into the crowd. "This is a great opportunity for all of us to unite. Actually, I'm not sure if any of you women saw this, but we had a few girls from the crowd supporting this event today. It was beautiful, and if you all turn around, there is a picture of them."

The shift of heads and bodies filled the auditorium, and then I saw a picture of the girls with their posters. I smiled. This was working. The crowd roared and hooted and hollered for them, and some even stood up.

"This is the type of unity we need in all of our society," she added, but then took long strides until she found the corner of the stage. A group of women were walking out.

Christy Pepper began one of her many other speeches that I was sure she had in store for today, and then let the girls – one by one- read off the words in the back.

Lyanna and me ended up playing rock paper scissors shoot with each other, and I was winning partly because Lyanna only played with paper, but then the sound of one woman grabbed the whole rooms attention.

" Before I say my pledge, I want everybody to know that we should give thanks to Christy Pepper," the girl suggested. Everybody in the room started to clap and cheer; the woman on stage clapped pugnaciously , and said a few words that I wasn't able to understand.

"Christy Pepper is a wonderful woman, is she not? I mean who wouldn't want the job of controlling our lives? Which is why, I- AM- NOT- PLEDGING- MY- ALLEGIANCE- TO- SOME- UNGREATFUL"

The guard immediately rushed onto the stage armed and ready, blending in with the stage. I was further back from the stage, so I couldn't see her face but to put it in perspective, she looked the size of an inch from where I was sitting.

I could tell she was putting up a fight with the guards because of all the shoving and kicking she appeared to be doing. The other girls on stage had broken away from their straight line. Now there was a big huddle of girls' stage left, and the one girl on stage right.

"TAKE HER AWAY!" Christy Pepper roared. After her command, the guards distressfully tried pulling the young lady off stage.

"Sorry, everybody," Christy Pepper apologized to us. "As you can see, this is what happens when young girls are crazy."

"STOP PUSHING ME!" the young girl was screaming. She was almost off stage, but the fight she was putting was unbelievable. She had three guards attached to some point of her body, yet here she was, still on stage.

"Again, I am so deeply sorry you all had to witness that exemplarily act of defiance. I would really try not to do that, for your own sake," Christy Pepper apologized. The young girl was off the stage completely, and the microphone was being passed back down the line while the girls recited the pledge.

I shook my head, and pretended to listen to the rest of the pledges, until my mom went up. Although I did listen to her speak, I slowly drifted back off to sleep where until I was being woken back up to leave.

~

The pledge that we all made to Christy Pepper was

one of the best things that happened to our Subdivision, and one of the worst. Everybody was very happy as the month of February left, and we entered March and the people were also nicer; even Christy Pepper seemed to be jollier.

The girl who had rejected saying the pledge was executed yesterday morning that made me very angry because she had no funeral, and nobody mourned over her death.

The worst part was that W.A.R. got caught together. It was the early morning of March while we were all sitting together at lunch in Subdivision Square.

As the group of girls sat at the table, we were all discussing what we were going to do in May, and what roles each of the girls would play. One of the guards had been there the whole time in the room, listening to us, and then at the very end, took Ms. B away.

The guard took her outside to her car while all of us girls sat anxiously waiting to see what would happen. Because Ms. B new the guard well, the guard let her off with a warning, but Christy Pepper would still be informed about it.

When she came back inside the café, she informed us that the meetings would have to stay on the low down. We all exhaled with relief, and the meetings of W.A.R. came less frequent the next few months.

CHAPTER 12.

The cold, winter months melted away, leaving the warm of spring to only have one place to go. The snow was no longer in piles along the streets, and the trees were no longer leafless. They were fuller than ever covered in green leaves with flowers and bees and apples and bunches of sun.

My mom was getting huge; it had gotten to the point that she could no longer hide the fact that she wasn't pregnant anymore. Her stomach was the size of several basketballs, but they didn't bounce she moved, and she had frown out of all her clothes.

She had decided to call the baby, Chris, if it was going to be a boy, but the only people she told were Ms. B and I. She told everybody else that her baby was going to be called Angelina, a very girly name that nobody would suspect what my mom and I truly thought; however, we still didn't know the sex of the baby, but my mom wanted to find that out at the last minute.

It all changed one early morning in may, though when I woke up to my mom's constant pushes and pulls of my body to get me out of bed. I didn't have any time that morning to do anything; she had just raced me out of bed and into the car.

"Where is this place were going to?" I asked her, cracking my window.

"It's near the hospital, probably fifteen miles away," she answered.

I didn't know where that was, but didn't bother telling her; she would explain it to me into a full-length detail and add extra details, and would probably forget that she told me and say it again; I didn't need to hear that right now.

The building we were going to- when we finally arrived- was big, and tall. It extended way beyond the height of building I was used to, and had a variety of different shaped windows that peaked about – what seemed like- ten feet tall. When I stood next to the window, it was easily double my height, and I am not even five feet.

The outside of the building didn't look like a hospital, but the inside couldn't be anything but one: white walls, white floors, and people in white jackets.

I drifted off into one of the deserted corners of the waiting room while my mom checked herself in. Situated right in the corner was some kind of funky chair, something I had never seen before; but it looked old. The chair's seems were tearing and coated in cobwebs. Maybe it was curiosity, but I sat in it.

It felt comfy, but used, and old; sort of like home. The color of the chair was distorted so that I couldn't tell if the chair had once been black or navy blue, but the tag on the seat said brown. It also said lazy boy chair.

What the heck was a lazy boy chair?

I didn't dare get up or move, the squishy cushion was much more comfortable than the couches I had at home. I lay back, put my hands down at my side, and then jerked my hand away; something cold had touched it.

What ever I had touched slipped in between the cushion and armrest of the chair, so I reached my hand in between the crack, and pulled it out.

This object was skinny, cold, circular, and gold, and I didn't recognize it. I had never seen it before; one side of this circular thing had a face on it, and the other side had a building.

I think this was called a penny, but I wasn't sure, and if it was, I had heard from a myth that it meant good luck;

I needed it right now.

"Ms. Amanda Yards?"

I looked up only to see a doctor looking at my mom.

"Are you ready?" she asked. My mom nodded and then found me, and jerked her head towards the doctor. I followed.

When we entered the hospital, we veered to the right where several elevators were, and hopped into one. I could only see the doctor's and my mom's back, but I saw her push the third level, and then the elevator lifted.

We stepped out of the elevators and the doctor's office was right in front. My mom lay down on this bed-like contraption with a screen next to it. When the doctor came in, my mom's face lit up, and she even hugged her. I stared, but didn't want to be rude, so I asked her who she was, which was probably ruder.

"I am Doctor Penny," she answered me, a happy-go-lucky smile decorating her face. I smiled back too, and felt the weight of the penny in my pocket rocking around. I didn't need to worry about this appointment, because whatever was going to happen, we would be okay,

Incognito

"Your mom and I have been friends for years," Doctor Penny explained, shoving latex gloves on that were, coincidentally, white. Her golden locks matched her golden eyes that blended in with her golden skin. Overall, her appearance gave her an aura of kindness, and I didn't feel the need to hide things from her.

"Just lye down right on the bed, if you can do that for me, and stay still," Penny ordered. She lifted my mom's shirt up carefully to expose her round belly, and rubbed some clear gel-substance all over it. In an instance, something gray had popped up on the screen.

The gray picture was moving, and a gasp from the doctor alerted us. "It's a…" she hesitated, but she didn't dare the sex of the baby; I feared that it was a boy; she let that hanging for my mom to conclude. But my mom already knew it.

"There's baby Chris," my mom cried. She lifted her fingers to touch the screen.

The doctor looked really worried, but as quickly as she could, she printed out a blurry image of the child and turned the screen off, then left the room.

"What about the baby?" I asked my mom.

Would Penny turn my mom in? Would she not get to keep it?

My mom laid a hand on my arm and whispered, "Don't worry Sam. Penny is one of my dearest friends. She is safe."

I don't know how much that calmed me down, but my mind relaxed, and I sat down on a chair against the opposite wall. As Penny came back in, my mom was using the towel that sat at the end of the bed that she was laying on to clean her stomach.

"Here are your pictures of- have you picked out a name for her yet?" Penny asked. I raised my eyebrows in disbelief.

Was she confused?

"Angelina," my mom answered sincerely.

Did my mom believe her?

"Well, you can be on your way now. Just sign these papers, and I will see you in a few weeks for the birth of Angelina. Best of luck to you!" Penny handed my mom a few papers, the pictures, and as nicely as she could, hurried us out the door.

"Don't you find it a bit odd that she changed the sex

of the baby?" I silently asked my mom, holding the elevator door open for her.

My mom shrugged, as if it was no big deal. "Well," she said. "I think she was doing that for her own protection. You do understand that she is letting us go, and I have a baby boy in my stomach."

We had met several times with Ms. B over the past few months, planning on how we were going to get the boys out, and the best part was that we gathered a few more people who were going to help. Now we had a total of twenty-one people; it was growing.

There had been no more riots and out bursts in my subdivision, so no more people had suffered executions. But, there were more laws in place. Not only had Christy Pepper put in the law about pledging our allegiance to her, but she had also put in a new order about having all of us take certain tests that would indicate if we were against her, or not.

The tests began yesterday, and would be happening up until Women's Revolution Day. The only thing I needed to do was to meet up with W.A.R; we couldn't be caught like the first time, and we barely made it out if it wasn't for Ms. B.

She was the one I was most worried about.

~

The next day I met with Ms. B, my mom, and the rest of W.A.R. group; it was imperative that we meet up because I wouldn't see most of the group until Women's Revolution Day. So, Lyanna, Ms. B, and myself helped spread the word about the meeting, and by third period, all group members of W.A.R. knew about the it after school; Ms. B was holding it in her class room.

Because I had Ms. B's class at the end of the day, I stayed in her classroom and helped move the desks around for the meeting. Mary, Rebecca, and Lyanna stayed too, since they were in my class, and before the first member arrived, all the desks had been placed in a circle.

Ms. B sat tranquilly at her large desk, pretending to do work, while I sat to her right, and Lyanna sat to her left, us being her wing women.

"I'm going to take attendance now," Ms. B announced as the last girl entered her classroom. She shut the door silently while Ms. B started calling all our names and gathering a few papers.

After she knew all of us were here, she passed around an article called 'Women's Revolution Day' for all of us to 'pretend to be reviewing'. This was just in case we had a visitor and they wanted to know while we were all at school; we had to be safe, since it had happened before.

Ms. B cleared her throat, and waited for the talk among our group to settle down, and began speaking. " What is the main goal for us meeting today?"

"It's to review Women's Revolution Day. There is not much time until it's here," Olivia answered. She was the newest member to the group, with curly, dirty blonde hair, and voice that reminded me of a mouse.

"You are correct," Ms. B agreed. " And why are we going over this article?"

"Because we need to make sure were all on the same page before the parade," I answered. I looked around the room as all the girls nodded their heads. Ms. B was nodding too.

"Yes, indeed we do, Miss Yards. Why-"

The sound of the door handle turning alarmed us. There were a few gasps in the crowd, but I shouldn't have been one of them because it was only a few of Christy Pepper's guards.

This was about to get interesting.

"Sorry, mam, but we're here under Christy Pepper's orders. We were told to inspect the classrooms for any suspicious activity. Do you mind if we sit in here for a few minutes?" one of the two guards asked. They came in anyway, regardless of what our answer would have been, and sat in two empty desk closest to them.

"Proceed," the other stated. They each pulled out notebooks and pens and started scribbling stuff down. Ms. B looked at all of us, smiling weakly.

"Okay, class, back to what we were discussing. What are the characters going to do up until Women's Revolution Day?" Ms. B asked us. I had to say, it was an odd question worded weirdly, but Ms. B wasn't going to be able to do any better, especially with the guards sitting on the opposite wall.

" Well- uh- the characters are going to stay out of the way, and round up their followers," a girl named Macy said. She was sitting next to the guards nervously.

"What does she mean, 'round up their followers?'" a guard asked. She looked up at Ms. B who kept her face as straight as possible, looking at only the guard.

"Well, if you had read the article, you may know," she responded coolly. Ms. B flipped through the article, and proceeded to ask us different questions, and eventually, the guards finally left due to a call they received. "Thank you for letting us sit in for a bit," one of acknowledged, waving to us as she disappeared through the door. When the door shut, we all exhaled.

"Okay everybody," I shouted to get everybody's attention. "The only reason why I called everyone out here was because we need to decide how were going to do that tests."

"Well, I have already taken the test," Ms. B informed us, while heads were turning. She stood up from the desk, and slipped into the circle of all the desks.

"All you need to make sure you do is concentrate on how great Christy Pepper is, okay?" she told us.

She didn't' say much after that, and then dismissed us from the meeting.

~

I walked home by myself in the dark counting the stars, and by the time I got home, my mom was there waiting outside. She then informed me that I would have to do the test today.

I froze.

"Are you sure I have to do it today?" I asked her, hoping she would tell me that I could just go back inside and relax.

"Sorry, Sam, but if you plan on going back to Incognito tomorrow, you need to have been cleared."

I hung my head and opened the car door. I didn't say much to my mom as we drove, because I was trying to focus on how great Christy Pepper was.

My mom drove me to Subdivision Square, and we went to the furthest building to the right. There was a line of people stretching from the building to the fountain.

"Is this for the test?"

"I believe so, Sam. Why don't we get in line," my mom answered. We passed through the gate and got in line behind an older woman while other people got behind us.

The only light outside was the moon, shining high up in the sky laminating the faces of people waiting their turn. Most of the women here looked frightened, although they had no reason why since they didn't believe what I did, or was going to do what I was about to do.

Their faces grew more frightened as the guards filed up and down the lines taking names and information that I couldn't hear. When they finally made it down to me, I was about to enter the building.

"Okay, What's your name?" the guard asked rudely. I didn't have to look to see who the guard was; I knew it immediately.

"You know my name," I said to Mal. Her black hair and black eyes blended in with the night.

"I wouldn't use that tone with me, Samantha. I will

be at Incognito tomorrow when you go, watching your
every move," she retorted back. She left without asking
any more questions, and started questioning another
person.

" Samantha, lets go," I heard a voice calling me. I
hadn't noticed that my mom and me had made it to the
front entrance. I waved goodbye to my mom, who stepped
awkwardly away from the crowd, as I was directed into the
building.

I couldn't tell what sort of building this was, but it
was one-story, and had more rooms than I could count
walking into it. The guard walked me straight back down
the scarcely lit hallway and into a small room; one green
chair sat in the middle.

"Just take a seat there," the guard instructed me,
leaving the room. She slammed the door behind her,
letting me by myself in a small room, and a chair.

I couldn't do anything in the room except sit in the
chair, so I did, with my knees up and shoes off. I quickly
put them down again, just in case the government thought
I was trying to go against them. Even though I was trying
to go against them, I didn't want them to know that just
yet.

"Sorry to keep you waiting," a voice called. It was a young woman in a black suit that walked in, and stood in front of me.

"Okay," she began. "All I need you to do for me is describe what you see in the following pictures I show you. Does that sound good?"

I nodded my head while she pulled out several pictures from her jacket she was wearing. After, she pressed a button on her watch, and showed me the first picture.

It was the color blue in many different shades; the bottom was bright blue, and sky blue, and the color of the ocean blue. Then it morphed into a dark, rich blue, that I couldn't tell if it was black or blue. I laughed.

"I see the color blue. Am I supposed to see anything else?" I asked her, while snickering.

"Dig deeper," the lady urged me.

I thought for a minute, and staring at the corners of the page, and still had nothing.

"Okay," I said. "I see a person trying to figure something out."

The lady nodded her head, and flipped to the next picture, but she still looked like she was a little skeptical of my answer.

The new picture was completely different. It was a birds – eye type of picture, and was a city that had buildings rising higher than where the camera was positioned. The street below was filled with many dots that I assumed were people.

"I see a crowd of people," I stated.

"What do you think they're doing there? What time period do you think the picture was taken in?" the guard asked me. I looked closer and a bell inside my head clicked.

This picture looked like it had been taken during a speech, but not just any speech, a Christy Labelle speech. The buildings reminded me of the buildings from my family's video of one of her speeches too. At the corner, there was a bright, yellow flag – or square, I couldn't tell- at the bottom of the picture, and a small space surrounding it with nobody there. That must have been where Christy Labelle was giving her speech.

"The picture was taken a few years before the

Women's Revolution was finalized. This must have been taken during one of Christy Labelle's speeches she gave," I proudly stated. I sat up a little straighter, my confidence, boosting. But the guard looked shocked.

"How did you know that?" she asked, checking the photograph to make sure it was the one I said it was. "Have you had some knowledge on this issue before?"

I didn't know how to respond, so I kept my head forward and didn't say anything. She scribbled a few words on the back of the photograph, and flipped to a new one.

This photograph was funny looking. It had a teary-eye in the center of it, and images of birds flying around it.

"What is this picture saying?" the guard inquired. She held the picture right in front of my face muttering to her while I thought.

"It has to do with a person and freedom," I told her.

She scribbled something on the back of this picture too, and then escorted me out of the room, down the barely lit hallway, and out into the night where my mom was waiting, bored. The line of the people to take the test had only increased since I had been outside.

"How was the test?" my mom asked as we started walking back to our car.

"I don't know. The lady kept writing things down. What if I said something I wasn't supposed to?"

My mom didn't answer my question, but just kept her mouth shut

CHAPTER 13.

Incognito

I woke up with butterflies flying all around my
stomach, and not the silly little butterflies that flew around
my stomach the first time I departed for Incognito, but the
ones that pounded the insides of me, because they knew I
was about to do something I may regret. I pushed them
aside (because I had gotten really good at that), and got
dressed. Even though it was the spring, Incognito still
required me to have long pants and long shirts, so I put
my plain jeans and long-sleeved t-shirt on, and went out
into the kitchen to see my mom.

" I m-made you b-break-f-fast," my mom stuttered. I
could tell that she was really nervous. For me, or for her, I
didn't know.

"It's okay, mom. This plan should go smoothly," I
promised. But honestly, I didn't know how it was going to
go. I just smiled and ate my cereal.

When I finished, I grabbed my suit once again, and
my extra bad that had a few tools I would use. I made sure
I had all my things and my mom and I left.

"Just remember to be very careful," my mom warned

to me while she was driving me to the school.

My stomach churned even more.

But this is I wanted.

This is what I was going to do.

No turning back.

The school came into view and my mom put the car into park. She gave me a long hug and whispered in my ear, "I have faith in you. You can do this."

She held me a little bit longer, and then there was a tap on the window; it Ms. B. She looked very stressed, but she was smiling. My mom rolled her window down, and Ms. B whispered a few things in her ears. I couldn't hear them, but I was positive that it was about the trip we were about to take.

I stepped out of the car, and waited for Ms. B, who lagged behind me a few minutes. When she was done talking, my mom drove away, but screamed out her window, "Good luck!"

I stood on the curb with Ms. B, waiting for the other girls to arrive. Luckily, the girls that were coming with us were on our side, or not for a side.

, the bossy girl who has brown hair, arrived after me. And then Rebecca showed up, but she didn't say much. Lyanna's essay was surprisingly picked, so she was coming too. And the last girl, I didn't know her. She wasn't in my class, and I had never seen her before.

"Okay, so we're all here, aren't we?" Ms. B asked. She counted all of us under her breath, and then said, "Grab your luggage and bring it this way. We're taking my car."

The five of us girls followed Ms. B to her car, which wasn't hard to find. The parking lot to the school was small because most people didn't have cars. Ms. B's car was probably the biggest of all the cars; hers could fit nine people.

We piled into the big van with our luggage tightly tucked away in the back, and then we took off.

"Okay girls, our main goal this next three days is to tell everybody about what were going to do," Ms. B confirmed with us. "We are taking Michael, Jeremy, and Samuel out on the last day, and bringing them out of Incognito. We will use them as leverage during the Women's Revolution Day Parade."

We all nodded our heads in agreement.

If only Ms. Doe knew what we were about to do, I thought.
If only Christy Pepper knew what we were about to do.

I laughed silently, and stared out the front of the van.
I was next to Ms. B, who was driving the car, and Lyanna
was next to me in the front. Behind us was a row of three
seats where the other girls sat, bickering about what their
favorite clothes were.

"I can't believe I'm doing this," Lyanna panicked. Her
hands were flying around by her sides.

"Can't believe your doing what?" I asked.

"Yeah, that's funny. I can't believe that you actually
have me participating in this nonsense!" she waved her
hands all around the van, the girls in the back, and me.

"I'm going to jail. I'm going to have to pee on a cold
toilet seat and wear jump suits of a gross color. And they
probably wont even fit me..." She babbled to herself, and
to anyone who would listen, but that would include me
because I only had her sitting next to me.

"Oh well," she concluded, lightheartedly, and then
dozed off.   *She's the type of people who need to be running the
government,* I thought. *People who don't care, and people who can
just ' oh well ' it off.*

192

When lunchtime hit, Ms. B pulled off one of the exits for us to find a place to eat, so we ended up eating at a small hamburger joint. When we went in, we ordered, and sat at a round table. The television was on, and newscaster was on.

"We have just received word that the head of First Division, Christy Pepper, will be participating in next weeks Women's Revolution Day Parade in subdivision five. Christy Pepper, why subdivision five?" the peppy newscaster asked. The camera panned over to the left where Christy Pepper was, and zoomed in on her.

"Well, I cannot say much, but if you haven't already heard, we have been having trouble in Subdivision five lately- like the passed few months. What I can tell you is that there are rumors flying around about something that's happening in subdivision five this year, so I would like to be there," she said.

I looked at Ms. B who looked as pale as a ghost, or as white as white could get. The rosiness of her check had vanished, leaving a slight redness where they should be.

"Were okay," Ms. B soothed us, or maybe it was for herself, I wasn't sure.

The hamburger was really good, and I devoured it fast. Being the first one done left me with no options but to go outside and wait by the van, so I did. Clouds started rolling in, but thankfully the rest of my group made it back in the van in time; it was pouring ten minutes later.

The rest of the ride took forever. The rain made Ms. B driver slower, and she took the wrong exit off the highway. That delayed us about half an hour, but once we were back on track, the ride was easy.

We took a deserted road that led us down to Incognito; my heart leaped as it came into view again. Even though I was looking through the gate, I could see the building wider than ever, stretching from the west side forest, to the east side forest, and rising high above the trees. My lips parted into a smile.

"What're you so happy 'bout?" a woman angrily asked.

I didn't see her at first, but when I looked up, I should've known. It was Mal. How could I have forgotten about her.

"That fact that in three days, I will be away from you," I said coolly. Ms. B had her window rolled down, her arm dangling out the mirror. She gave me thumbs up; Mal didn't notice.

"Well move along then, and stop crowding the gate," she sneered.

After the gate crept open, Ms. B rolled right through. At the front of Incognito, there were five boys waiting, and Samuel was among them. I didn't know the others, but I think these were the few boys that the girls in the car were observing.

This was it.

Ms. B pulled slightly off and over to the grass, where she put the car in park, and looked back turned to all of us.

"Okay," Ms. B sighed. "This is the last time that we can all talk as a group and I want to wish al of you good luck, and to remember our plan."

We all opened our doors and tumbled out of the van while two guards grabbed our suitcases. While the guards disappeared into the building, Ms. Doe was leading the group of boys towards us.

"Welcome back!" Ms. Doe cried. Her skinny arms rested on her hips, and then embraced us in a hug.

"Well, I guess there is no reason to explain everything to you girls… you know what to do…"Ms. Doe said no more. She walked away with Ms. B and we were off to do what we came for: spread the news.

Samuel was in the way back of the group in his shirt and shorts, and found his way to the front. He smiled the smile that reminds me of my mom, and we went straight to work.

The first thing I had to do was persuade him to do it, but that didn't take long. We were sitting back at the basketball court watching the other guys play.

"Okay, so there's really only one reason why I am back," I stated. I looked Samuel right in his blue and green eyes, and took a giant breath and said, "I am determined to free you, and all the guys here, and all the guys everywhere."

"Well you do set your standards high," he commented. He laughed a little and stood up stretching.

"So will you help me?"

"That is a redundant-?

"So will you help me?" I repeated, but with a stronger

voice.

"Yes."

I looked away from him and into the sky so that if the guards saw me, they would possibly think that I was angry with him, or disgusted by him, or both. I didn't look back at him, but rather stood up and had my back face him, and spoke to him like that.

"We will have to warn the others," I hissed underneath my breath. I turned slightly towards him so that he would hear me better, and so that I could keep my voice low still

"Well tell me what I need to do, so I can do it," he said back. I heard the shifting of an object and the scrapping against the pavement to find Samuel in front of me.

If Ms. Doe had been here while I talked to Samuel, then I would have been hung right here in front of him. My conversations of rebellion would be my cause of death, and she would feel no remorse for doing so.

We continued our conversation there for a while, and then designed a path around Incognito where we followed it and walked it a million times. Even though my legs were aching and screaming in distress, my body didn't want to stop, so we kept going.

The end result of our conversation was that we would call the mission FLOD for Freedom Long Over Due. The women here shouldn't notice the word FLOD, because it isn't even a real word, and the acronym could be used to talking in front of the women. Something inside of me was tingling with happiness and joy.

By the time dinner rolled around, I was allowed to eat it with Samuel. He brought me to a big table with many different boys of different ages. I felt strangely out of place, sitting with a table chock full of boys, but I loved it, and that scared me.

I sat next to Samuel who introduced me to the other boys, shoving the food into their mouths. Most of them didn't want to have anything to do with me, so they didn't speak, but the one guy sitting next to me did.

"Name's K9," he said through his food, staring at me with his blue eyes. I could tell he was probably a tall person, judging by how much of his body was above the table versus mine, but he also looked familiar.

But how could be familiar? I thought. *I have never seen him in my life before, so how?*

In a shaky voice I said, "Well, I want you all to help me-"

"Were not helping you girl!"

"Yeah, what makes-"

"STOP IT!" Samuel screamed at them. Half of the table of boys was angry; their nostrils were flaring, and their ears were fuming. The guards around the dining hall looked at our table, and started walking to us. I sat and held my breath, hoping something would happen, and then a big crash over on the opposite side startled all of us, and all the guards' minds went to that. I exhaled, and looked back at Samuel.

"Listen to her," he ordered at them. He flexed his muscles after he put his arms on the table. I didn't know what kind of gesture that was supposed to be, but a few of the guys settled down.

"Give me one good reason why I should listen to her," one of the guys demanded. His black eyes seemed to only darken as his anger rose. He too put his arms on the table and flexed, but his muscles were not nearly as big as Samuels.

Erin L. Monaghan

"I'm his brother," I admitted. The boys around the table nearly chocked on their food, and when they weren't choking on their food, they busted out laughing, slamming the table with their fists, food flying everywhere.

"I'm serious! And there are two other boys here that belong to Ms. B, my teacher!" They stopped laughing, but were still looking at me like I was crazy.

"What game are you playing at girl?" the boy across from asked. His arms still were on the table, and his plate of food a foot away from him. I glanced around at all the other guys and they had also all pushed their plates away from themselves.

"The point is, I want to free you guys," I confessed. A second of silent and deep thought followed, but K9 broke the silence.

"Well, you know I'm game for anything. I'll do it! Have nothing better to do in this life, right fellas'?" he laughed a bit, as if joking, which I'm sure he was based off his tone. The one guy in front of me still didn't get it, and left the table looking very angry; although the other guys nodded their heads in agreement, and I felt good for that.

"How do you think you're going to do this?" K9

200

asked. He looked at me with his blue eyes so big and bright, with a smile the size of a watermelon. I don't know how I was going to thank him because he was being so genuinely kind to me, and I didn't know if I deserved that.

"Well, I am getting Samuel out-"

"Who's Samuel?" he asked.

"E5," I answered. "Anyway, I am getting him out of Incognito in a few days when I leave, with two other boys."

"Why?"

"Women's Revolution Day Parade is almost here, so I will use them when it happens. Do you think you could spread the word?" I asked him.

"Yes, what ever you need," he answered. "I'm so glad someone is finally going to try and fix this." He looked at me and smiled, leaving the table. The rest of the table left without saying anything, so it was just Samuel and I.

I stared at Samuel while I sat in thought. The dinner conversation with the boys shocked me, and had gone so well. I had not expected for them to react so thrilled as they did, which meant maybe I could accomplish something; maybe something could happen, and boys would walk freely again.

Samuel stood and motioned for me to follow him, and soon we were in Samuels' tiny bedroom again, where the bare walls looed barer than ever. His bed was still against the corner of the wall underneath the ventilation system, but he had shifted his dresser to the wall beside it.

"So, how do you -" Samuel's voice echoed in the distance, but I wasn't paying attention; I had bigger and better things on my mind.

"Why don't we go up there," I proposed, interrupting him. I gave him an apologetic face – the one with my eyes all big and a smile that's small- and looked up at the ceiling. "I think we should go through it. It can hold us, right?"

His eyes widened as did his smile, and he hopped up on to the bed, shaking the dresser on the opposite wall. After he retrieved the thin, little string, he pulled down the door, and he demonstrated how to get up in it. He reached his hands inside the ceiling, and jumped so high that his whole entire body went easily into the square.

Incognito

It looked really easy, so I tried. And then I tried again because it was slippery. All in all, my chances of getting through the square in the ceiling were looking bleaker and weaker.

Samuel's hands were up there getting ready to grab ahold of me whenever I would make my way through the square, but it never happened, so I decided to try one last time. I bent my whole entire body so that the weight of me rested in my legs, and in the air. I bent low, and then sprung high –as high as I could- in the air, and through the ceiling I went.

My hair got stuck in the square in the ceiling, but other than that, my ride through five feet in the air was good; better than I expected. Samuel didn't even have enough of a chance to grab me when I came through because I was flying so fast. But before I started exploring, I waited for Samuel to close the door; I would hate to see the punishment he would receive for this.

Once he did that, I had my chance to look around, not that there was much to see; I was hunched over on my butt in a vent system that lead to who knows where. I heard a clicking sound, and saw that Samuel had a little tiny flashlight that looked no longer than my index finger.

He flashed it in my direction, burning my eyes for a
second, and flashed it down the vents; they seemed to
stretch on for miles; three days wasn't even going to cover
it. But we would try.

I sucked in my stomach while I propped myself on
my side and plastered myself against the vent so that
Samuel could start leading the way through them. He easily
passed me (while crawling still), and hobbled down the
vents; I trailed behind.

Every ten feet or so, there would be an air vent; one
on the left, and one on the right, that you could see
through. Not that I was going to look, but I could see
through the vents into all the boys' bedrooms, which was
weird.

We crawled for what seemed like eternity, and then
we can to some kind of ventilation intersection. We had
the option to go up, down, to the sides. So, without even
think, we chose up. I was eager to see Ms. Doe's office
again.

There was a latter we had to climb in order change
levels, so I went first climbing while Samuel went beneath
me, just in case I fell. He felt like I would probably do that,
but because we are related, wouldn't he too?

Incognito

When I made it to the top of the latter, I had the option to go forwards or backwards. I chose to go straight and realized the vent systems were kind of like a maze. But this maze was trickier because you could go up and down and right and left and every other direction in between. It was crazy.

Samuel was right behind me, but I lead this time. After a few minutes of crawling – and we hadn't gotten very far- a voice came traveling passed us. I asked Samuel if he could hear it, and he could, so we stopped and listened.

"I know, I think that idiotic girl of yours is up to something," a voice bitterly concluded. My gut told me it was Ms. Doe, and better yet, it was. She had it out to get me.

"She has been acting suspicious lately," another voice chimed in, agreeing with Ms. Doe. I was surprised; it was Ms. B. "What are you checking?"

I crawled closer so I could hear them better, and found a vent that I could see through. Samuel and I pushed our faces together, and judging by the angle we were looking from, we were on the floor of Ms. Doe's office.

"I just want to be sure of a few things- I mean, what if she knows that E5 is her brother? And tonight she had dinner with K9. What is happening?" Ms. Doe sighed, exasperated, with anger in her voice. She was on the other side of her lavish desk, but it was difficult to see her; she had a stack of papers in front of her face, so that I could see her fingernails stained with pink.

Was K9 another brother of mine?

"Allison," Ms. B calmly said, putting her hand on the desk. "I am more than positive that Samantha knows her brother is E5. This is new to her – the whole boy and girl interacting thing we got going on. There is nobody else to tell her about this but you. Nobody knows but you."

Ms. Doe put the papers down, exposing her skinny, sallow face, and countered, "That still doesn't stop the fact that K9 and her were communicating this evening. What if she finds out that he is her dad? I mean, tell me what I'm supposed to do from there?"

I gasped, loudly, and banged my head against the vent, causing Ms. B and Ms. Doe to jerk their heads around. I covered my mouth with my hands, and held my breath; Samuel did too.

"What was that?" Ms. Doe asked. She stood up from her desk, and started heading towards her office door.

"I'm not sure-" Ms. B started to answer, but when she looked down, her face widened with fear; she saw Samuel and me.

"Actually, I bet it was some kids downstairs. You know I keep hearing some loud banging noises in my room…" Ms. B fully responded. Her voice was really shaky, and she was motioning her hands to leave. We did, without any hesitation.

We crawled viciously through the vents while Ms. Doe's voice angrily crawled through the vents with us. With me in front, and Samuel in the back, we were able to make it back to the intersection quickly, but we didn't know where they would be right now. My legs and arms were feeling like Jell-O I as I positioned myself to go down the vent, hoping I wouldn't fall, climbing fast and ferociously.

The floor of the vents below crept up on me, and then I had to remember which way I was supposed to go, because I didn't know. Samuel had a vague idea of which direction we had come from, so he picked backwards and crawled.

The same vents were popping up every ten feet, so I felt like he had picked the right way to go. And then miraculously, he found his door to the ceiling, and one by one we fell down.

I didn't have a chance to sit because Ms. Doe's voice came trailing underneath the door.

"WHO HAS BEEN UP ON THE FIFTH LEVEL?" she screamed. Samuel got underneath his covers quickly, and because I had nowhere else to go, I went underneath his bed. It was a really tight fit, but I sucked in and held my breath, touching the wall as much as I could.

The banging of doors could be heard from wherever Ms. Doe was. The banging got louder as she got closer to us, and then she was at Samuel's room.

"E5!" she yelled. The door slapped the wall and ricochet off the wall.

Samuel didn't say anything first, but I think he was trying to pretend he was sleeping. After a few seconds, the bed creaked everywhere, and he said, "Is it morning already?"

I stifled a laugh, and wondered if Ms. Doe noticed his tone, but she didn't.

"WHAT ARE YOU DOING?" she yelled. I could see her feet from underneath the bed, violently tapping the floor.

"Sleeping," he said groggily. "But not anymore!"

"Never mind, then," she spat angrily, slamming the door on her way out.

I let out a sigh, but then Samuel quietly whispered, in an almost un-audible tone, "Don't get out yet. She will be listening at the door for a few moments."

I did as he commanded, and lay underneath his bed for a while until I felt too sleepy to get up. But I knew I had to, and when I did, Samuel had already fallen asleep.

Before I left, I stood at the door leaning against it, watching him sleep. He positioned himself in such a way that resembled my mom almost exactly, with his head lying on his shoulder, and mouth tightly shut. His legs were pulled up to his chest, awkwardly, and all I could think about was my mom. It was almost as if she was here right now, just in a different form.

I slipped out of his room, silently closing the door, and wandered my way back to my room. The fourth floor was the most confusing; there were so many turns and places to end up, so you needed to pay attention. When I rounded the last corner I needed to before I reaching the stairs, there was a sudden noise, and a person. The figure was large and black at the end of the hall.

"Is that you, Samantha?" a voice called. It was a male's voice, but I didn't recognize it at first. But I didn't dare say anything, in fear that if I said yes, Ms. Doe was watching or taping me to use it against me. I leaned my whole body against the wall, flattening it, and hoped the figure would walk away, but he didn't. He kept drawing closer and closer to me.

"Why are you wandering the halls this late at night?" the voice asked. When the person got close enough for me to see who exactly they were, I exhaled with relief, because the voice belonged to K9.

" Just taking a midnight stroll," I responded. I doubt he thought I was telling him the truth, but he went a long with it.

"Me too," he responded. My eyes widened, not that he saw, because why would he need to be walking around this late at night?

"What are you doing out so late?" I asked him.

"Thinking," he answered. "I was just wondering about a few things."

I didn't say anything, but rather just let him think a loud. Although his hair was blonde, he looked almost exactly like Samuel.

"Well," he said. "I'm just going to go, okay then. I'll let you be. Good night!"

K9 turned around and walked in the other direction, and disappeared into the blackness of the hallway. I lifted the door handle to the stairs and quickly walked down a flight of stairs and came to my floor. It wasn't nearly as pitch black as Samuel's floor, but it was dark. But I found my way to my room, and my bed, and fell a sleep almost instantaneously.

My sleep was undisturbed, but it I had had one of the most unnatural dreams I had ever had before. Ms. Doe's voice kept ringing in my ears telling me, "K9 is your father," and kept repeating it to me. She explained it to me that it was the boy version of a mother, and then I concluded that I had completely lost it, and was drenched in sweat.

Erin L. Monaghan

CHAPTER 14.

I woke up feeling refreshed and relieved from the night before, but dirty too because I had sweated. I took a quick shower and made my way down to breakfast so I could meet Samuel- who was already dressed and ready to go for the day-, but he had graciously waited for me to come down so we could eat together.

All through out the morning as we ate, I couldn't stop myself from thinking about K9. I was finding it harder and harder to block my thoughts out, so I cracked at the tail end of breakfast.

"About last night…" I began, hoping to trigger Samuels mind without having to speak it out loud.

"Yes."

"What's a father?" I asked him. I felt embarrassed because I should have known this by now- from him or from Incognito in general. I lifted my eyes to look at him.

"Well, the way that you came to be on this earth was by a man and a woman. A single part from a man is joined with a single part form a woman where the baby then uses those parts and is somehow created. They call the woman of the baby the mother, and man of the baby the father," he explained to me. He said it so easily as if he had practiced telling someone the story.

"So does this mean that K9 is the other man who helped make me?" I asked him. It was making sense, but then I was getting angry too. Here at Incognito I had a brother and a father that I had never met until now, and my world had lied to me; I felt betrayed.

"Yes, I think that would be right."

I finished the last bite of my eggs and stood up from the table. So many questions were entering my head. *Did he know? Does he know? Is K9 Samuels dad too?*

I paced around the table for a minute, thinking. I didn't know what to do next, or how I should process this information. But what I really felt like going up to Ms. Doe and screaming at her, but I refrained myself. The rest of the people in First Division were going through the same thing I was, but they weren't aware of it.

"How about I show you something?" Samuel asked me. He motioned for me to follow him, and soon we were out of the dining hall. He brought me to the large, circular room that I first saw when I came into Incognito. I saw all the colorful doors, and Samuel picked a red door.

"Were not supposed to go in there," I gasped. I

pulled his arm away from the door, and he looked at me, laughing.

"You know were also not allowed to spy on Ms. Doe and be in her office without her knowing, but you see how well that worked out," he countered, opening the door just enough so that we could slip in. "It's okay," he murmured. "Of all places, this one isn't the worst to come to."

When Samuel turned the light on, a huge library lit up, with hundreds of shelves lined with thousands of books. There were at least two huge step latters that had at least twenty steps to each of them that we would be able to get the books.

"What's so special about a library?" I asked him. The only thing that struck me as something to look into was that it was organized by color, which sort of reminded me of what Lyanna would have done. She sure did like to sort colors.

"This library is just a small collection of books from before the Women's Revolution. This is the real deal," he explained. He started pulling out books and reading them off to me. "We have War and Peace written by Leo Tolstoy, Romeo and Juliet by William Shakespeare..."

Erin L. Monaghan

"Is this where you got Dear John from?"

He nodded while I lost count of all the books he was listing to me, and then I lost myself in all the books. After a while, I realized all the books had one common aspect to them; they all had both women and men in it. All I wanted to do was read them, because what I was reading today were about girls, and that was it.

There wasn't a window in the library, but I could just feel like time was escaping us, and that the day was coming to a close. Dinner would be soon, so eventually we came to the conclusion that it was time to leave. We made sure all the books were lined back into place, and then cautiously departed from the room. I probably shouldn't have taken another book, but I grabbed the first one I touched and slipped it into my jacket.

~

The last remaining twelve hours passed quickly. Before I knew it, I had eaten dinner with K9 and Samuel, read some of the book I took which happened to be Romeo and Juliet. Then the morning sprung up on me all of a sudden, and I partook in another sleepless night. I couldn't believe it! The past three days here had flown by so fast that I hadn't been paying attention, and yet here I was.

The feeling of emptiness and queasiness grew stronger in the heart of my stomach, telling me I shouldn't be doing what I was going to do today. All I wanted to do was leave safe and sound, but I had no idea if that was what was going to happen. My clothes were packed in my black suitcase and already in the van, and a couple of males helping me get the three boys out of Incognito were all ready. If only I was as ready as them.

I breathed in, and I breathed out. F.L.O.D. is all the males were talking about. It had been spread all through out Incognito, which made me felt good, and bad too. In an hour, we would be gone from this place and be on the road, but what would that mean for the rest of them?

I paced back and forth on a small square of grass where Samuel and I had been sitting on. He was still sitting, but I was up and had managed to dent the grass. My body was shaking and I couldn't concentrate.

"Were not going to know if we don't try," he said, trying to calm me down. It seemed to relieve some of the anxiety I was going through, but I was still pacing. Then I

217

felt a warm hand on my shoulder.

"Are you ready?" a voice whispered. Ms. B was standing as close as someone could get to me; I about smacked her in the nose with my head when I turned to see her.

"As ready as I can be," I answered. She grabbed my arm and pulled me away from Samuel as he shouted "good luck!" to me from a distance. This was the first step to the plan.

She walked me as far as she could from Samuel, so that by the time I looked at him when I turned, he was as big as my thumbnail. She brought me to the edge of the grass where it meets to the concrete where the rest of the girls were waiting.

Out of the five girls waiting, I found Lyanna sitting down on the ground plucking pieces of grass, organizing them from biggest to smallest.

"Why do yah look so nervous?"

She didn't stop sorting the blades of grass. She turned to get one glance at me, and then let her black, straight hair fall down again.

I didn't say anything back, I just pointed to the white van and said, "Oh boy oh boy I can't wait to get home!" She obviously hadn't caught on to my hint of the use of the word boy; she looked at me like I was stupid, and then said noting more.

Ms. B returned back to us only to have brought Ms. Doe and two guards with her, and Jeremy and Michael. Behind them, I could see Samuel lingering around getting closer and closer to us.

"Thank you so much, Allison," Ms. B said, giving Ms. Doe a hug. "This has been a very nice and informative trip my girls. I cannot wait to see what type of essays they bring to the table!"

"Yes, I too am looking forward to that," Ms. Doe agreed. She looked specifically at me, and quickly focused on something else.

"Well, girls, I will look forward to seeing you in a week. I-"

BANG. BANG. BANG.

The sounds of something crashing inside Incognito alerted Ms. Doe. She looked at the two guards, and they rushed off. Ms. Doe looked at all of us and shouted, "Safe trip! I must go see what that noise was," before she hurried along after them.

The next few minutes were the slowest minutes of my life.

Ms. B opened the back trunk where Michael, Jeremy, and Samuel jumped into the van, while I headed straight for the front seat with Lyanna, and the other girls found their seats behind us. In less than thirty seconds, Ms. B had found the time to help cover them up with suitcases and blankets, and get into the van and start driving. As I looked back at Incognito while Ms. B drove away, K9 was in one of the windows waving to me, and smiling. I waved back too.

When she got to the front gates, Mal and Carson were in their normal spots with their guns, looking straight ahead. They turned to face us, though, when our white van pulled up.

Ms. B rolled down her window slightly, so that Carson and Mal would hear her when she spoke.

"We are now leaving, myself, along with Samantha, Lyanna, Mary, Rebecca, and Elizabeth," Ms. B stated. Her voice was shaky as she spoke, but I'm not sure if the guards noticed.

A crash in the back of the car rocked the car, and we all turned to look, but nothing was wrong. Mal looked very irritated, and then sighed.

"Are you alright? What happened down there?" Carson asked. She looked at all of us in the van, and then jerked her head towards Incognito.

"I'm not sure. There was a banging noise and then the two guards with Allison went to find out what it was. We left as they left us," Ms. B explained.

"Well then don't look so nervous, I'm sure one of them boys is getting a good whippin' as we speak," Carson said, laughing. She hit the top of the van with her hand, and backed away.

"It's not like your hiding any boys in that van with you," Mal stated. Ms. B laughed along, and then said farewell to them. Lyanna, and the rest of girls and me stayed quiet. Nobody dared to speak until we were on the highway.

"That was close," Ms. B sighed. She looked at all of us and congratulated us. She then asked the boys how they were doing. I looked behind me to see if I could see them,

221

but they were still concealed.

I heard a muffled, "Good," from one of them, and then Samuel popped his head up.

"Michael and Jeremy, you can show your faces; the windows in this van are tinted, but there should also be some wigs in the back you can put on," Ms. B called to them.

I had to admit, the wigs looked pretty real. Samuel's wig was dark brown and fell well below his shoulders while Jeremy and Michael had red wigs. All of the wigs also had long bangs, and I guessed that it was probably to conceal their faces.

"Where did you get the wigs?" I asked Ms. B. The only time I knew that wigs were sold was during Halloween.

"I bought them a long time ago just I case I would need them like today," she answered.

I looked at the mirror in the van and saw that the three boys had their faces plastered against the windows looking out, even though it was just land.

"Do you like it?" I asked them. Nobody budged, but

Samuel did speak.

"It's beautiful," he whispered. He turned toward me and said, "Everything is beautiful."

I let him get back to looking through the window and just sat watching them watch outside. When we drove through the more populated areas, they loved it even more, and wouldn't stop talking about what they saw and what it was, because they weren't familiar with any of it.

For some strange reason, I felt the best I had in all my life. I felt accomplished and proud and didn't want this to end. I felt like I was on top of the world, and nothing was going to bring me down.

The trip back home was quiet and familiar. When we reached the roads and buildings we had known our whole lives, Ms. B instructed for them to put on some dresses, that way when we did step out of the van, people would be less likely to stare and make the conclusion that they were boys.

But Ms. B was going to minimize this because she started dropping us off at our houses. When we dropped Mary off at her big house in her rich neighbor hood, the same noise that banged the back of the car happened again. But like earlier, we turned and nothing was wrong. Samuel called from the back, "Don't look at me! Or Jeremy, or Michael!" The rest of us were bale to settle back down, and we continued on.

Next were Elizabeth and Rebecca, so we dropped them off together because they lived next to each other. Lyanna's house wasn't too far from theirs so then she was dropped off, and it was Ms. B, the three boys, and myself in the car.

I could imagine that my mom was at home waiting anxiously by the door with dinner on the stove cooking. And when we arrived at my house, that's exactly what happened.

My mom had one of the curtains drawn back so that I could see that she was reading. But when we pulled into the driveway, she didn't see us, which was good. If she had, then she would have gone nuts and started crying and screaming, and that would have caused attention.

I stepped out of the van and went to the back to grab my suitcase. On the side door, Samuel stepped out, and thanked Ms. B in his long brown wig and frilly dress. I waved goodbye to Ms. B and Jeremy and Michael, and they were off.

"You ready?" I asked Samuel, as we stepped up to the door. I knocked, and opened the door. As soon as we made it inside, my mom shrieked, and ran towards us, embracing Samuel in a big hug.

She was crying too much to talk, but I had I feeling I knew what she was thinking. I went to the curtains and pulled them closed, and made sure the rest of the curtains were closed in the house so that nobody would see inside.

"Well don't just stand there, lets go get dinner. I'm sure your hungry," my mom assumed. She brought us to the kitchen table and had him sit down, where she filled a gigantic plate full of everything she had and put it in front of him.

"Thank you, Ms. Yards," Sam said, picking his fork up.

"Don't you dare call me that," my mom shouted. " Call me mom," she said thoughtfully.

Samuel didn't know what to do, so I laughed, and then he said in a very hesitant-like voice, "Okay, mom."

My mom was beaming at her seat. She bombarded Samuel with so many questions, and then continued after dinner, and when we were in the living room. But I think he really liked it.

"Well mom, I call him Samuel," I told her, as we sat on the couch. I had forgotten to tell her that when we came in, but she was so fixed on seeing Samuel I hadn't told her.

"Well I think it is a wonderful name," she said gleefully. She was sitting next to Samuel with her arm around him, smiling and laughing. I was happy too.

"Well feel free to do –" my started saying, but then the TV turned on. Instead of seeing Christy Pepper, it was Ms. Doe.

"Sorry for this interruption, but four of the males have escaped Incognito!" she frantically said. Two guards joined in with her, Mal, and Carson. "We tried to keep it hushed up the past few hours, but we cannot find them anywhere."

Four people? I asked myself. *We only took three.*

Four boys popped up on the screen and I screamed. While Jeremy, Michael, and Samuel were on the screen, K9 was too.

"How did he get out?" I asked Samuel, looking at

him.

"I don't know!" he answered.

"K9 was last seen at outside of Incognito five hours ago, and probably hasn't gotten very far if he is outside traveling on foot," Carson informed us. She looked over to Mal, who's face was all screwed up; she was very angry.

"E5, F2, and X2 were confirmed gone just an hour before K9, " she abruptly stated. Then she turned directly to the camera and said, "Citizens of Subdivision 5-6- stay in doors! They are dangerous!"

A knock at the door made me jump high into the air; my mom did too; Samuel looked at me with his hands in the air, as if he was trying to ask me, "What do I do?"

"Go hide Samuel," my mom ordered. I pointed to my bedroom where he dashed off to while my mom called, "Be there in just a moment."

She scurried over to the door, and looked through the peephole. "Sam, it's the last boy from the TV" she screamed. "What should I do?"

"Open it!" I screamed back to her. I rushed to the door, and whipped it wide open. K9 stood outside looking very dirty and out of breath. I rushed him inside, checking to make sure none of the neighbors had seen, and then shut the door quickly.

"How in the world did you get here?" I asked him while we walked over to the couch. My mom had left briefly to retrieve Samuel and then joined us as I waited for his answer.

"Well," he began. "As I saw you leave, something inside of me told me to follow you, so I ran to the van and jumped on the side. I stayed holding on to the van the whole trip, and then I hopped off when you got to the first girls house. I traveled on foot from there."

As he finished, I stared at him in awe; what he did today was something that could have killed him. A strange feeling was growing in the pit of my stomach.

"Well I am very glad you're here," I told him. Then I turned to my mom and said, "I think you might want to know something; something that me and Samuel can tell you."

Her brown eyes looked at me inquisitively and she asked, "What might that be?"

I took a breath, holding Samuels hand, and said, "K9

is my biological dad."

At first, my mom looked at me confused, but as she thought about it, it became a reality. "You mean to tell me- this man in here- he is-he is the other half of you?" she asked me.

"And me too," Samuel added. I looked over to K9 who also was processing this information.

"So I am your father?" he asked me. "And I am his father?"

I nodded my head and couldn't stop thinking that this felt all too real. I had my father and mother and brother all in the same room, all under the same rooftop; this was unbelievable.

"I know it's a lot to take it, and you may not believe-" I started saying, but then my mom interjected.

"No, I believe you honey. This is-"

"Amazing," K9 finished her sentence. He looked around all of us and said, "I felt something when I looked at you Sam. And then I saw how you interacted with Samuel and knew it." He smiled, and then strangely gave me a hug. I had to note that this was the second hug I had received from a boy.

"Can he stay here?" I asked my mom. "He doesn't have anywhere to go, and if we turn-"

"Yes!" she answered. "Yes! Yes! Yes!"

I went over to her and hugged her tightly, then Samuel joined in, and K9 joined in too. We stayed like that, in a big ball, for a while, until I broke the silence.

"Well, K9, we ought to give you a proper name," I blurted out. We all broke away from the extended hug, sitting back down.

"Like what?"

"Why don't we name you Bernard, like the dog," my mom suggested. I nodded my head in agreement laughing, and then checked to see if Samuel liked the idea too.

"I like it, Bernard," Samuel said, nudging his elbow against Bernard's body.

"Well, Bernard, would you like some dinner?" my mom asked. "You must be exhausted and hungry for the trip you took today." As she said that, Bernard's face lit up.

"I would love some," he answered, standing up to

follow her.

As my mom went to the kitchen, she called, "Feel free to do what ever you want to do in this house. My house is Sam's is, and Sam's house is your house." Bernard and her had totally disappeared and all I could hear from the kitchen was her banging around.

"This is amazing," Samuel said to me, looking at everything. "I have only been here for an hour, and I already feel like I am home."

I smiled. I felt like I was finally home too, with a mother, a father, and a brother, by my side. The only thing my heart longed for was for freedom for my brother and dad.

CHAPTER 15.

I hadn't spoken to my mom much the passed week.
She seemed to act as if she was in a dream; she was happy
all the time, she sang a lot, and she even made more of an
attempt to socialize with people. It felt really good to see
her like that, but then again- was she not happy until now,
when I brought Samuel home? And when Bernard
appeared? I never stopped thinking about that, but I let it
go because I had other, more important things to be
focusing on.

The following week after getting home from
Incognito was chaotic and hectic and anything that falls in
between. Christy Pepper and Ms. Doe had made several
appearances on the news too. They had told everybody
that the four boys were almost captured, and that they
would be back at Incognito in no time. But nobody had
the minds like W.A.R, because besides us, everybody
believed them.

Everybody in my subdivision also was going crazy

because of the parade, which happened to be only two days away. I had lost track of time, and had completely forgotten about.

On Friday, I was in charge of pumping the yellow balloons and directing the different floats, but that didn't go over too well. I caused two people to break their arms, and one person to dislocate some body part on their body. By that time, I had called it quits.

I was also running into issues trying to hide Samuel and Bernard. They weren't allowed to come out of the house for starters, not that they minded. I would leave my house as late as I could in the mornings, and come back as early as I could to see them, and my mom, too, was mimicking my effort.

After a few days, we had gotten so used to Bernard and Samuel living in the house, that we started making careless mistakes. One of them was leaving the curtains wide open where all the neighbors – or anyone- could see inside.

"Mom- did you see that?" I had asked her Wednesday evening. Samuel, Bernard, and I were sitting on the floor looking at old baby pictures of me, and the single photo of him, while my mom was knitting. She looked up at me, and shrugged.

"No, what did you see?"

"Samuel –Bernard- go hide! I think someone saw you two!" I screamed. I bounced over to the heavy curtains and pulled them tightly together. A person standing in the middle of the street caught my attention.

My mom rose from the couch and meandered over to the front door where she peeked through the window. Nothing.

"I think your hallucinating," my mom suggested. She found herself back on the couch, knitting. I looked at Samuel and Bernard, and shook my head.

"Somebody was out there!" I whispered to them, and ask soon as I had, a knock at the door came.

"Excuse me, but Amanda? Samantha? Are you home?" a voice called. I didn't even have listen to it to know that it was Ms. Doe. She was probably here to snoop.

"Coming," my mom called. She walked as slowly as she could to the door as I rushed Samuel and Bernard into my room. I put them into my closet and had them each sit at the very ends of it. I pulled jackets and blankets over them to make it look like my closet floor was very messy. I could hear my mom talking to Ms. Doe in the front hallway, so I sat on the floor of my bedroom, grabbing the first book I saw, pretending to read it.

"And this is Samantha's room," my mom informed Ms. Doe. "Can I come in, sweetie?"

"Yes," I called, as she opened the door. Ms. Doe stood right next to my mom, taller than ever, in her six inch heels, and striking, bright blue blazer to match them.

"Why hello there Samantha," she greeted. "Lovely room you have." She came over to me, and gave me a hug. As we were hugging, I had the book behind her in my hand, and I realized I had grabbed Romeo and Juliet. When she pulled away, I quickly tossed the book onto my bed.

"Have you caught those creatures yet?" I asked her. I emphasized the word creatures hoping that she would catch that I 'didn't like the male species'.

"Well that's why I came to see you," she answered. Under her eyes were heavy, purple, bags that made her look paler and more tired than she should be. I think my mom noticed, because then she asked her if she wanted some tea to which she agreed to. While my mom left the room, Ms. Doe sat herself awkwardly on the floor of my bedroom.

"You haven't happened to see the boys around, have you?" She inquired. Ms. Doe pulled her hands onto her lap staring at me. Once or twice I could have sworn I saw her pull her eyes towards my closet, but I focused on not noticing.

"Here is the tea," my mom said, coming into the bedroom. The plate that she had the cup on was rattling fast, and then she suggested, "Why don't we go into the living room, so we can talk there."

Ms. Doe agreed and stood up. As she had her back to me, a sneezing sound from the closet startled me. Ms. Doe whipped her body around so she could see me, and right as she did that, I shoved my fingers across my face like I had sneezed.

"Sorry!" I apologized. "I always get colds around the times when the seasons change." She didn't believe me, but she kept moving along until we were back into the living room.

"I hope you can find those boys soon," my mom said, crossing her legs while drumming her fingers on the couch. "Unless they have found sanction, they're probably dead- or close too it."

My mom's dark complexion grew lighter by the minute as she lied blatantly through her teeth. She had never dared to even say a lie in her life, and here she was, chock full of them.

"You're probably right, they are probably dead," Ms. Doe agreed. She put her tea down, and then stood up.

"Well I must be off," she informed us. "I'm sorry if it appeared that I was coming in rushed, but I just wanted to let you know that just doing my job.

"Thank you for the tea," she thanked my mom. After a few minutes of chatting, she was out the door and walking to her car. I was able to relax and collect Samuel and Bernard again.

"She's gone," I called to them, entering my room.

'Thank goodness," I heard Bernard saying. "I thought we would never get out of there." He came barreling out of the closet with Samuel right behind him.

"That was a close one," Samuel said to me, as he stretched out his legs.

"Too close," I agreed with him. "Too close."

■■

The morning of the parade drove my mind wild. We had decided that Bernard would stay here at the house and that it would probably be safer too. He would be able to watch the news to see what was happening at the parade too, to keep tabs. So while my mom was getting prepped for the day, I was helping Samuel get into his disguise, and it was hard.

He was going to be on a float that had the statue of Chin it, surrounded by the people who ruled after. His outfit, along with Jeremy and Michael's, was the easy part. But I had to put enough make up on his face to conceal his maleness.

I took fake eyelashes and red lipstick and all sorts of make-up and decorated his face. An hour passed before I could say I was done, and then I pulled back, and showed him his face in the mirror. It looked pretty good. I had to say he looked pretty good.

"What have you done?" I heard my mom scream. She was standing in the doorway of the bathroom, mouth hanging to the floor.

"Mom, he has to be able to go out in public, remember?"

She nodded her head, and then reminded us to be ready in a few minutes. I laughed. I had not gotten ready myself, but I rushed. Within five minutes I had a yellow frilly dress on and white heels. I combed my hair so that it fell in deep waves against my back, and threw on a little bit of mascara. I grabbed my shoulder purse and walked to the front door where my mom was waiting with Bernard.

"I'm glad you could finally get ready. Maybe we'll make it on time this year," she joked. "Shall we go?" she added. She opened the door while me and Samuel filed out, and stayed back for a few seconds. She was talking to Bernard inside, but soon enough she was back out the door. The curtains were drawn over all the windows, and the door had been locked.

"Okay, so I'll let you and Samuel off by the Belle

building?" she asked me. She pulled out of the driveway slowly, and made her way north on the street. From the end of the street, we could see thousands of yellow balloons waving in the air, and thousands of people walking to the parade.

"Yes," I answered, but all the people distracted me. I had been to every single one of the celebrations every year, but not once did I remember this many people.

I think we were the only people who had chosen to drive, because there was no traffic; however, it did make it really easy for my mom to drop us off at the building.

She put the car in park next to the curb in front of the Belle building, and grabbed my hand. "Good luck," she whispered. Then she did the same to Samuel, and whisked away into the crowd.

In the distance, I saw thousands of people holding balloons, little girls running around with their faces painted, and some were dressed up – probably for the parade is what I assumed. A few more figures dressed similarly to Samuel got my attention, so we followed them. It was a tough chase because of all the people crowding the streets, but Samuel was able to see a little bit above the crowd. When we approached the similarly dressed people, it indeed was Michael and Jeremy.

"I'm so glad to see a familiar face," one of the boys yelled at Samuel. He clapped Samuel on the shoulder, and then pointed to a float that glowed in the distance. "We have to go their now. They need us," he said.

I wished them all luck, and found myself getting sucked in by the crowd. I saw many new faces and old faces, and some that didn't look like faces but they were faces as they all pushed into me, making me dizzy.

Just to make it worse, someone spilled something blue on my dress, so part of me was yellow, and then some parts green. I didn't have time to get angry, but rather I left and went to the outskirts of the road where I could see the floats.

There were so many floats lined up and ready, so I just sat and waited. Soon enough, a band erupted into the beautiful harmonies of a hundred different instruments, playing our anthem of First Division. The first float started, and the rest started following.

I saw a few really cool floats go by, emitting a hundred colors of yellows and blues, but they were very boring in terms of how enthusiastic the people were on the floats. But when Samuel's float went by, it got the biggest clap.

Because I knew that three of the eight people on the float were boys, I could pull them out. Samuel was the center of the fountain, positioning himself into different poses every minute. Michael and Jeremy were a few of the smaller statues below him, also changing, while a few girls danced around the float.

I couldn't tell if Samuel had waved at me, but he waved at something, so I waved back. While I stood alone, I couldn't help but wish Bernard were here. Even though it was celebrating the event where women took the men over, he still would have enjoyed all the people, because he was that type of person.

The music played loudly, and then after many floats- I had lost count of them- had passed by, I felt a hand on my shoulder. "Are you ready to go?" the voice asked me. When I turned, I saw Ms. B standing in a dark blue concoction of a dress and shorts all in one. I eyed her outfit, but she said nothing; she was just waiting for my response.

■■■■■■■■■■■■■■■■■■■■■■■■■■■■■■■■■■■■■

"Yeah- I guess I am. Don't we need Samuel, Jeremy, and Michael?" I asked back.

"Yes, they are on their way to the Belle building. We are going to meet them there," she answered. Ms. B grabbed my arm and pulled me through the fighting crowd. Once we had pulled ourselves through, the Belle building came into view, with three boys standing beneath it in costumes.

When we got up to them, Samuel opened one of the heavy doors for us, and we all clambered through; there were several guards waiting inside for us.

"Okay, we have them here," one of the guards said into a walkie-talkie. Then she looked at us and said, "Just wait a moment please, and then you can follow me."

The guard took out a few papers and jotted something down on it. While she did that, I circled the whole room to get a panoramic view of the place and was struck by how gorgeous the place was.

The walls were marble, the floors were marble, even the pencils and pens lying out on the desks were marble, or at least they seemed to appear marble. The theme in this room- or building, I should say- was yellow. Besides the marble, everything was yellow.

"Okay, lets go," the guard, said, interrupting my thoughts. She plowed through the rest of the building with our group barely keeping up with her. Then we came up to the staircases where we climbed four flights of stairs, and a hundred steps later, we entered a long hallway, which was just as beautiful as the one downstairs.

The hallway was so beautiful that I felt like I was walking into my own death. Maybe I was, but it felt too real to be true. At the very end of the hallway there were two big windows and a door that led to somewhere, which I was going to guess was the outside. And just where I thought we weren't going, we did. The guard came up to the doors, and then led me through.

I held my breath as I passed through the door, the sun biting my face.

CHAPTER 16.

I stepped onto a balcony high above everybody. I turned behind me and saw the guard disappearing back into the building, while Samuel, Jeremy, and Michael stayed inside to. Ms. B walked out with me, and when I turned again to face the crowd, I noticed Ms. Dow and Christy Pepper.

The balcony I was standing on was at least four stories high, very wide, and made out of marble. I don't know how old this building was that I was standing on, but the intricate designs etched into it on the side made me guess that this wasn't a creation from women, but of the men. All I can say was that it was beautiful.

Below me were thousands of people dressed yellow with yellow hats and yellow balloons and yellow everything. They were all clapping and cheering on the parade, while I could only see the tips of the glorious floats passing by.

Christy Pepper, the Head of First Division, Ms. Doe, and Ms. B were the only other people with me up in the balcony, the rest of the people were in the crowd.

"Eh-hem," Christy Pepper coughed. She cleared her throat once more to grab the rest of the crowd's attention, and when they all did, she started speaking with her happy voice.

"Happy Women's Revolution Day everybody!" Christy Pepper shouted. She threw her fists in the air, and joined the cheering. "On this day 117 years ago, Women finally claimed their independence! We were finally set free from those filthy creatures of- well never mind them. I will have to tell you that ever since 2021, they have been locked up! Our guards have done an impeccable job keeping them contained. Lets give a round of applause for our guards!"

The crowd busted out into claps of thunder and roared and cheered. I snapped my fingers in disgust to what she was saying, but did no more.

" Before I hand the podium over to Ms. Allison Doe, I wanted to take a moment in silence as we honor those courageous women like Christy Labelle, my great-great-great-grandmother, and the others who fought so courageously," Christy Pepper ordered. She bowed her head, and the thousands of little heads in the crowd did the same, until she backed away and gave the podium to Ms. Doe.

"Thank you, Ms. Christy. And thank you everybody," Ms. Doe began, paused, and looked out into the crowd. " As the manager of Incognito, I will say, our guards do such a great job, but it is because of our great Head of First Division, Christy Pepper."

Ms. Doe and everybody fervently clapped again. Christy Pepper smiled and waved her hand high up in the air, and bowed. I felt like I could vomit.

"Well, as some of you- but not all of you- know, we had the seniors go to our Subdivision's facility, Incognito, to do some observations of the creatures. Everyone was required to submit essays of their own after the observations, and the winner would give it today, in front of all of you. And without further or due, please give a

welcome hand to Miss Samantha Yards," Ms. Doe
welcomed.

I stepped up to the podium, put my flashcards on the
top, and gazed out into the crowd. My heart fell.

No, it didn't fall, my heart dropped.

And it plummeted.

There were so many people out there, watching me,
listening to me. I knocked the microphone, sent it
tumbling down, and burped.

Breath, I thought. *Just breathe.*

And be confident.

"Hi," I greeted everybody. They all laughed, myself
included, but my voice was so shaky.

"I guess you have heard that I won the essay, right?
Um, I have. We can all assume- or should I say, one of Ms.
Doe's mottos is that in order to sustain nature, their needs
to be balance. Can we all agree that balance and nature go -
um- hand in hand?" I asked everybody. The microphone
flickered a little bit, but came back.

All across the land I saw people's heads shake. I

breathed in, I breathed out.

" We should really commend our government because they have done such an incredible job covering up our nations past, you know? But they're-"

The microphone made a fuzzy sound, and went completely off. When I said the word 'wrong', nobody heard it except for me. The crowd screamed in anger. The microphone had been unplugged by Ms. Doe, who then swiftly came to me and yanked my arms.

"Don't you do this, girl!" she screamed at me. "I will not have you disrespect Christy Pepper!"

Her grip only tightened on my arm.

"No, it's okay Allison. Lets hear what Miss Yards has to say, after all, she is the expert on this topic, is she not?" Christy Pepper sneered. The microphone was plugged in again with more static-like noises.

"Sorry for the interruption," Christy Pepper apologetically said, but she didn't really mean. She chucked the microphone back at me with a side sweep of a smile.

I glanced over t

"The government is wrong," I shouted. The crowd gasped the biggest gasp I had every heard. "They never have been right, they never will be! Remember that balance and nature thing I mentioned a few minutes ago? Well, guess what, we as a group are apart of nature whether you want to believe it or not, which means there needs to be boys and girls!"

Over the roar of the crowd, nobody heard the shriek Ms. Doe gave or the shouts of Christy Pepper when they heard me say that boys and girls needed to coexist.

Christy Pepper and Ms. Doe were also too shocked by the news they didn't notice Jeremy, Michael, and Samuel slipping through the doors to the balcony. Jeremy and Michael grabbed Christy Pepper while Samuel took Ms. Doe, injecting them with something that would put them to sleep.

This was going as planned.

Samuel came out and stood by me, should to shoulder, while Jeremy and Michael dragged the two bodies inside the building.

"Before I say anything else, did you like the floats?" I asked, and their was an uproar of excitement. Cheers exploded all over.

"Just so you know, someone very important to me was on your favorite. The float where Christy Labelle was in the middle and the dancers dna

"Everybody," I shouted. I paused until I had everybody's attention. "This is Samuel, my brother."

Samuel stepped forward so everybody could see him. At first the crowd didn't notice because he still was in his costume, but as his the crowd looked further, gasps could be heard from all over. I couldn't hear what they were saying, but the confusion and anger on their faces could be read easily.

CHAPTER 17.

I woke up in a silver room- no- it- it was gray; all around me was gray: the walls, the ceiling, the chair that I was sitting in, even the door handle. I didn't know where I was, but then all the events came flooding back into me.

I could remember speaking to the crowd of thousands of happy people celebrating Women's Revolution Day.

I could remember when I showed them Samuel, when the crowd went silent, when I couldn't tell between their shrieks of terror and cries of approval.

I could remember when the guards all below took there guns and aimed them at me, and when Samuel dove in front of me when the bullet soared through the air.

Where was Samuel?

My body froze in panic. I needed to find him. I stood up, slightly, but then wobbled from left to right.

"I wouldn't suggest standing up right now."

I know the voice I was hearing was a woman's voice, but where was it coming from, I didn't know. The gray door opened, exposing the brightly lit hallway behind it. Oh how I wish I were out there with Samuel.

The woman was in a gray suit that covered her hands and her feet, and she had gray mask on her whole head. The only part of her body I could see were her eyes, but that was it. They were gray too.

"I envy you," she blatantly said. She took off the mask on her face, and out popped Ms. Doe. "I don't know anybody willing to sacrifice so much for something they're not going to win."

The body suit hung very loose on her skinny body while she paced back and forth in the small room. Her crazy red hair hung below her chest, clinging to her ribs.

"Do tell me, what did you think you were going to achieve by doing this?" Ms. Doe asked me. She continued to pace, staring me down.

"Do tell me, what do you think you're going to achieve by questioning me right now? Because I'm not saying nothing to you," I spat back. I kept my face in the same expression, and smirked.

Ms. Doe scoffed and let the room, slamming the door. It rattled the mirror on the wall in front of me, and behind it, a light came on.

She was in there watching me.

~

Several hours later, I still found myself sitting in this room. Ms. Doe hadn't come back in, but I could hear her voice on the other side of the mirror, no doubt having her watch my every move. But just for her sake, I'd walk up to the mirror and make faces at her, then walk back to my seat and put my head back on the table.

At one point, I remember a slight pinch, and a lady in gray swaying to both sides of me. My arm felt sore and went limp, and I fell back into a deep sleep.

I don't know how long she planned on having me in there because I was hungry, but soon enough a superintendent brought in some food. All I can say about it is that it was stale, and the food at Incognito was much better, and that was saying something.

Ms. Doe eventually came back, looking refreshed and pampered. I didn't have any idea about what time is was, so it could have been early morning, or lunchtime, who knew, but judging by Ms. Doe's appearance, I guessed that it was the morning.

"I am so happy that you are awake now," she chimed. She had a bag of food with her, and she started pouring it out all over the grey table. It looked like a feast. She had brought hot rolls and cakes and meats and potatoes. My mouth started watering.

"You have been saying some crazy things lately, Sam," she noted. She set two plates – thicker than her- on the table and started distributing the food. "I was beginning to worry. But you don't go start worrying; it has all been cleared now. You have been cured!"

As much as I would have liked to not eat the food, I did. My ribs were clawing the insides of my stomach screaming at me, and I may not have looked like I had been deprived from food, but I felt it. I scarfed it down, licking my fingers, the bowl, even the napkin. Ms. Doe took her time, watching me peculiarly.

"I knew that the minute you started talking about you-know-what that you were mentally ill. I don't know what triggered it, but it's not like it happens everyday. Only a small percentage of people here in the First Division get it, so it's understandable that someone like you would have gotten it," she calmly stated.

I'm not mentally ill, I thought. *She has it wrong. I know what I saw and what I did was real. The horror that struck her face that day —whenever that was- was real, and by the looks she gave, utter shock.*

"Thanks, but no thanks. I am most definitely not ill," I sarcastically said. "Actually, I was wondering where your room was, and where I could get my hands on a visitors pass?"

I leaned back in my chair, and pushed my plate away from me. Ms. Doe didn't flinch, nor say anything, or even purse her lips up into a confused ball of pink wrinkles on her face. But I smiled, and I let my facial expressions show and mix and confuse her.

Ms. Doe's black eyes sunk, and her mouth curved, slightly. She folded her hands neatly on top of the table, and continued to watch me.

"Your mom is waiting for you, outside, through the doors, right now. She has even said it herself that a mental illness is what you have had all along. I don't know what game you're playing, or what game you think you're playing, but give it up," she gasped. "Stop this nonsense."

She let her hands fly passed her face and into the air, carelessly. Her voice was calm and quiet, and even sounded kind. She knows just as well as I know that this "mental illness" of mine is really the "carelessness" of her.

"Please stand up and walk slowly. The medicine we gave you might make you a little droopy, and you may walk on a slight angle," Ms. Doe warned. She stood up and went to the door and held it wide open for me.

The hallway I stepped into was brightly lit and long. The hallway was yellow and happy, and had many other doors that went off into who-knows-where. If I had known that I was at some mental place, then I might have actually liked where I was.

Ms. Doe stepped in front of me, and guided me through the hallway. We took a series of turns through doors that broke off, and found ourselves into the entryway of wherever I was at. My mom was pacing in the room.

Her eyes were tired, and saggy, and red. She didn't appear to look as if she had slept at all in the past few days, and she probably hadn't. Her curly brown hair was clipped into a small bun in the back.

"Oh sweetie!" my mom cried. She ran to me and embraced me into a long hug, followed by a few tears.

"I was so worried about - you'll never guess- they are safe," my mom gasped. Her tears were huffed and puffed and her whispers were very muffled. I didn't know what she was saying.

"Do you think I could go walk outside with Sam? Just

for a moment?" my mom asked Ms. Doe.

Ms. Doe's face wore an expression of disgust. I knew she didn't want me to go outside, but I had a "mental illness" so I was allowed to go out for my wellbeing.

"Don't stay out too long," she warned. "Be carful of what you say. We have some eavesdroppers here."

My mom pulled me through the sliding doors of the building, and whisked me away.

The sun was somewhere in the middle of the sky, dancing on the horizon. The moon, on the other hand, was far on the western part of the sky, racing to the top. The air smelled fresh and felt clean, and the hand of my mothers on my shoulder felt like I was at home.

"Samuel is okay," she whispered into my ear. "He is at home with me. He's watching Chris."

She had the baby?

"When did you have the baby?" I asked her. I could feel the anger rising inside of me. I was supposed to have been there to see the baby; I was supposed to have seen the way my mom's eyes lit up when she held her son.

"I did. And I'm sorry, I couldn't control him," she

apologized in a soft whisper. She glanced around herself to make sure nobody was with us, and whispered, "Ms. B is with her sons right now, and we've even recruited a few more people regarding this situation."

Her face was glowing; her tan skin was shining; her eyes and smile seemed so pure, it reminded me that of a baby.

"How about that "mental illness" of mine?"

"They were going to take you away to jail, and-" her whispers were growing faster, but then a voice cried, "take her away."

I whipped my head everywhere to find the source of the sound and two guards came running towards me. I stayed with my mom, our backs together. One guard was coming from the south, while another guard ambushed us from the north.

I couldn't see who was behind the masked figures, but both of them grabbed a hold of me, dragging me away. My mom was screaming and crying in the background, and then something – or someone- hit my head. I began to fall back into the same rickety sleep, as before, only this time, I was a criminal in the eyes of my world.

Incognito

~

I don't remember when I came around, but when did, boy did reality sink in. I was in a room, surrounded by nothing.

The blank colored walls were surrounded by nothing.

The table I was sitting at was surrounded by nothing, expect for a peculiar woman with bad taste in fashion sitting directly in front of it. She handed me a circular mirror and asked me to gaze in it, and to tell her what I saw

But I saw nothing.

I kept looking harder and a face appeared: my face. It looked like me, with the same messy brown hair that couldn't decide if it wanted to be curly or straight; with the same changing eyes of blue and green, that reminded me of a sea; with the same white face and rosy cheeks that made me look like a clown.

I don't think I saw what she wanted me to see, so I told her that I saw me; the same me that I saw last year;

the same me that I have always seen. But she didn't like what I saw.

She tore the mirror from my hand and called me some ugly words that I would never repeat. She yelled at me and hounded me with questions about a boy named Samuel, whom I did in fact know, but wasn't going to say a thing; therefore I endured several hours of this woman screaming at me.

The woman stood up from the chair, frazzled. Her once tamed hair was now sticking out in every direction; her shirt that had once been tucked into her skirt was completely pulled up and out, dangling below her butt. She paced the small room we were in, muttering to herself about the punishment I was going to get when she finished, but In reality, I did nothing wrong. She was to blame; the government was to blame; everybody that had helped push where my world is today were all-wrong.

The woman knocked on the old door in the corner of the room, and too guards appeared. She pointed towards me, and muttered a few things to the guards, where they started grabbing my arms. Then they pulled me down the hall, into a cell, and left me.

Now I was in a different room, surrounded by

nothing.

The walls that surrounded me were a color of nothing.

Now I was sitting on a small bed, instead of chair to a table, which was surrounded by nothing.

I didn't have the woman though on the bright side to this dull room. But I could hear her laugh echoing through the halls, and I could almost hear myself laughing too.

I stared out the three-inch thick bars that lined the cell I was in, and let my mind wander the halls that I couldn't wander freely just yet. Out in the hall, my mind only found one solution to my problem, and one conclusion.

There are some things in life that can simply not be talked about. It is possibly one of the most difficult concepts to deal with, especially when you have mind like mine, swimming with questions that I cannot ask, and answers that I do not want. But eventually, it gets a little bit easier.

It becomes easier to block out the stupid remarks people make, just simply because society tells them to.

It becomes easier to go with the flow, even when you don't want to.

But it becomes easier to ditch the status quo and ask the questions you want, and get the questions you want. I have learned that so delicately the passed year that nothing matters in anymore.

"What's wrong with you?"

My heart almost dropped out of my body, for when I turned, I had no idea that there was a person in here with me. I peeled my face from the bars, and saw a girl who was leaning awkwardly against the wall.

"Well what's wrong with you?" I asked back.

"I asked you first," she retorted. She was thin, with stringy brown hair that was really long.

"Fine," I answered, crossing my arms against my chest. "I rebelled against the government, and just gave a speech about boys. You?"

"Oh- you know, the usual," she explained, stepping forward. "I was angry with the guards, and struck one of them." Then she laughed and made some punching gestures in the air. "I don't know, I've done it a thousand times before, but they just realized to now put my in jail?"

She stretched out her hand to me saying, "Nice to meet you. What's your name?"

"Sam," I answered.

"Well, Sam, its an honor to meet you," she said, bowing. "My name is Shelly, and I am your worst nightmare." She smiled a wide smile, and dragged me over to the wall.

"You," she paused. "And me, should definitely speak when we get out of here. I can be a part of your group. You do have a group, don't you?"

"Yes I do. It's called W.A.R., and stands for Women Against Revolution. It would be great if you joined," I answered her.

"Count me in," she said. Then she put her hand up and did a fist bump with me. She then started talking about everything we should do when we get out, and I couldn't help but smile.

I shouldn't be this happy in jail, or wherever I was right now, but I felt like this was going to happen. I felt like the men would soon be back in the society.

I turned my head to my worst nightmare while she vividly described what she did to the guard, and I just hoped and prayed that Samuel and Chris were safe at home. I had no idea if they were or where they weren't. But as I sat there listening to my worst nightmare, hope and faith were building inside me, and I had the best sleep that night than I had ever.

ABOUT THE AUTHOR

ERIN L. MONAGHAN IS Beautiful, Drop Dead Gorgeous, Wonderful, Amazing, Outstanding, Intelligent, Creative, Musically Gifted, Talented, Superb, Above Average, Well Rounded, Sweet, Kind, Keen, Fabulous, Clever, Inventive, Quick, Tranquil, Decisive, And above everything, Modest. The list could go on and on, but she wanted to stop because she is Modest. She is the type of role model everybody needs to pay attention to. She is the type of girl that understands life. Heck! She is life. She also has other attributes, like her skills with learning instruments, and drawing, and singing, and calling bingo. These activities she does really helps create her dynamic, well-rounded self. Please take a moment of silence for her.

With all respect,

The Author.

www.ingramcontent.com/pod-product-compliance
Lightning Source LLC
Chambersburg PA
CBHW030424290526
45786CB00001B/121